process
VISUALIZATION

process
VISUALIZATION

AN EXECUTIVE GUIDE TO
BUSINESS
PROCESS
DESIGN

NORMAN LOFTS

wiley.com

John Wiley & Sons Canada Ltd
22 Worcester Road
Etobicoke, Ontario
M9W 1L1

National Library of Canada Cataloguing in Publication

Lofts, Norman, 1947-
    Process visualization : an executive guide to business process design /
    Norman Lofts.

Includes bibliographical references and index.
ISBN 0-470-83197-9

    1. Production planning. 2. Business planning. I. Title.

HD30.28.L63 2002   658.5'03   C2002-904391-3

Production Credits
Cover & interior text design: Interrobang Graphic Design Inc.
Printer: Tri-Graphic Printing Ltd.

Printed in Canada
10 9 8 7 6 5 4 3 2 1

Contents

Contents   **vii**

Preface

Do you remember the movie "Fantastic Voyage," where a man was put into a capsule and then miniaturized and injected into a human body? As the capsule travelled through the body, you could see how the body functioned. Some scary things happened on the journey, but what a memorable experience it was to explore the inner workings of the body and see what happens inside the human machine. Today, of course, miniature cameras are often used in medicine to explore the body. But that movie, back in 1969, made you feel that you were actually there—inside a person.

In 1992, an article appeared in the *Harvard Business Review* entitled "Staple Yourself to an Order." The article captured my imagination and remains a strong influence in my work today. The illustration accompanying the article shows a wide-eyed executive travelling down a conveyor belt with a customer order attached to the lapel of his suit. The article pointed to the need for executives to experience how their people, business processes, and systems handle, or mishandle, their customers throughout the entire Order Management Cycle.

Executives need to experience what is actually happening inside their processes and not just rely on what anyone else thinks is happening or wants to believe is happening. Executives need to see their organization from the customer's perspective. By tracking each step of an order through the complete process, executives gain insight into their business as it actually operates today. This simple exercise allows anyone to experience firsthand what is working well in the As-Is state and what areas offer opportunity for improvement and change.

But how can you experience a business process that has not yet been implemented? How can you be sure that a proposed new design for systems and processes is the right design? How will the proposed new business process design support your new e-business strategy and its accompanying business model? How will the promising new technology enablers support your people and processes as they strive to give your customers better service? You could better answer these questions if you could somehow staple yourself to an order and travel through the To-Be business processes and enabling technologies.

Architects today are in the fortunate position of being able to take their clients on a virtual tour of a proposed new building. Using specialized software, a building can be created, allowing you to travel through halls, up stairways, and into rooms; you experience the feeling of being inside the structure. Consumer and industrial products are also designed today with 3-D computer technology. But business processes are not solid objects; they cannot be modelled or simulated like a building or a car. Is it possible, though, to somehow fly through the activities that people and systems perform to experience a proposed business process design that may very soon service your customers?

Visualization has always been a powerful way for me to figure out how things work and how they could be made to work better. Some years ago, when I was a pre-sales consultant demonstrating Manufacturing Resource Planning (MRP) and Enterprise Resource Planning (ERP) systems, I would take people through the flow of a process and explain how the software could be used to better support its activities. Although the software had the latest features and functionality, these alone never seemed to be the key to convincing potential clients about the merits of the system. But I sensed that when they understood how the complete process was going to work, their eyes would light up, they asked more questions, and an interesting dialogue about their issues would develop. My experience is that people gain a deeper understanding of their business processes when they can visualize them. This raises their comfort level and confidence to begin a change initiative. Change means uncertainty, both for the organization and for the individual. Careers can be propelled forward, stalled, and even lost, depending on the outcome. Executives want to be confident that their initiatives will succeed.

People remember the outlandish and the absurd rather than common, everyday events. Most people react strongly to a visual experience as is evident in the popularity of movies, videos, and plays. But let's face it, business processes can be pretty dry and boring. The challenge has always been to find a way to make them come alive. Process Visualization rises to this challenge to capture people's interest and imagination. It has made business processes come alive for executives because they can see the processes unfold before their eyes. It has succeeded in providing the capsule that takes you inside your systems and lets you watch as they perform various automated activities. Process Visualization lets you staple yourself to an order and travel along with it through your proposed To-Be processes and enabling technologies.

You will read more about how your people become actors and use the concept of live theatre to perform the design of business processes. This is the sizzle that captures people's imaginations. As well, you will see that Process Visualization has another important aspect. It is the solid foundation for business processes design, and it gives your design team building blocks and a common language.

The concepts presented here have been developed and refined over a number of years and through various consulting engagements with organizations. The work has always focused on the business processes and technologies supporting supply and value chains. The organizations were ultimately looking to implement new technologies to replace older systems. In some cases, these new systems were the catalyst for examining the business processes. In others, the business requirements to increase supply chain capacity, lower costs, and improve customer service levels drove new business process designs and the implementation of new systems.

You will read about how a major North American retailer used Process Visualization to launch the initial business process design project of their change initiative. This program in excess of $200 million will transform their supply chain when it is fully implemented. Everyone involved in this major business change initiative needed a way to express his or her design ideas, test innovative approaches to solving issues, and be assured that the design was "right." Using Process Visualization, the team and executives were able to experience their proposed new business process designs before the technology implementations began. They gained the confidence to move into the technology implementation phase of the change initiative with an approved process design.

Process Visualization is the result of developing concepts to provide organizations with a better way to design business processes and understand what will happen when their major business change initiatives are enabled with emerging technologies. There will continue to be refinements and new ways to make business processes come alive. These will come through working with innovative organizations that are willing to experiment and try unusual concepts that have the potential to make them more successful in their business change initiatives.

Acknowledgements

A book starts as a tangle of ideas and thoughts that are shaped over time by discussions with the many people who know your work. As the manuscript takes shape and more colleagues take time to review it and discuss their suggestions, it begins to feel like something concrete is developing and, perhaps, other people would like to see the project succeed. This gives you the resolve to move forward. When the work to publish the book begins, you start down a whole new path of working with the people who will turn your manuscript into a book.

My first acknowledgement must go to Kristine Freuden-thaler—a colleague, client, and trusted advisor throughout the writing of this book. Her insight resulted in the concept of writing two books, this executive guide and an accompanying practitioner's guide for project teams. Kristine, a vice president at a major North American retailer, spent valuable time and energy on this book while she was involved in the implemen-tation of a major change initiative. Her encouragement was key in my starting this project; her unfailing good humour supported me through its formulative stages.

I have developed the techniques of visualizing processes over many years with a variety of clients and have been able to experiment with and refine these techniques because of the strong support of clients who looked for innovative ways to design and communicate processes. I am grateful, therefore, to a number of senior business and IT executives, including Pat Sinnott, Lesley Page, Geoff Frodsham, Paul Jovian, Rick Gray, Rob Ramsey, and Cristine Prattas, at a retail organization; Norbert Tauchner, CIO at Westburne and Medis; John Weaver, President and CEO of Abitibi-Consolidated; and George McPherson, CIO of Maple Leaf Foods.

The resolve to stick with a developing visualization approach on the part of the people who manage the day-to-day activities of a major change initiative was crucial. I would like to thank two such project managers for their support and commitment: Dave Fieghen at a North American retailer and Mary Flaifel from the OGC project at Abititi-Consolidated.

There is a long list of process design team members who embraced Process Visualization and added their voice about how to improve the techniques. With the fear of leaving out some names, I would like to thank: Mike Bleau, Carmine Bosco, David Bunn, Fouad Chalabi, Heather Chapman, Paul Doris, Beverly Fox, Irene Glazema, Bruce Harper, Maria Kalatzopoulos, Josh Leitch, Terry Mathews, Gerry Munshaw, Jerome Ryan, Sylvia Waseem, and Irene Wilson.

Thank you to the colleagues, clients, and friends who spent many hours reviewing the drafts of the manuscript. I am indebted to you. Critical thinking on structuring and positioning came from Bruce McGillivray, President of Baxter Renal Europe; Tim MacDonald, President of A.T. Kearney Ltd.; and Gary Huggins, Malcolm & Huggins Search Partners. Specific comments and ideas focused directly on supply chains were provided by Baxter Corporation's Serge Maltais, VP Supply Chain and Brent Hodgson, Director Supply Chain; John Leavitt, VP Operations at Irwin Toys; Jim Eckler, President and CEO of Progistix Solutions; Greg Lashbrook of G-Log; and Paul

Drinkwater of PricewaterhouseCoopers. Others at Baxter Corporation whom I would like to thank for their comments include Barb Leavitt, President; Mary Parniak, CFO; and Jeff Bakker, Business Analyst. Others who contributed their thoughts include Paul Vaculik of Celestica, Bruce Hiatt of Staffopolis, Al Saipe of KPMG, Tony Targa, an author and educator, David Shaw of Digitel, Jerry Crawford of RBC Dominion Securities, and John Ruffolo of Deloitte & Touche.

I am indebted to Karen Milner, Executive Editor at John Wiley & Sons for believing in this book. I am grateful for the dedicated work of Elizabeth McCurdy, Abigail Brown, and Nancy Carroll.

Finally, I want to thank Lisa Wood, my partner, for her encouragement and continual support throughout the writing of this book. Her writing skills were critical in producing the many drafts of the manuscript. Without Lisa's dedication to take my developing thoughts and often-convoluted writing and transform it into understandable phrases, I doubt that others would have taken the time to read the manuscript.

I have learned much about processes by writing this book about them. I will be forever grateful to all those people who helped me throughout this personally challenging time.

Introduction

The Business Process as a Journey

Before you start to read this book, consider this analogy; it will give you a way to think about why it's important to focus on business processes at the start of a business change initiative. You will see that determining the requirements for supporting technologies is tightly linked to the design of the business processes. There are three analogous elements to consider:

- The journey is the business process.

- The vehicle to take you on the trip is the enabling technology.

- The planning for the journey is the business process design project.

Now, imagine that this summer you have a very specific travel goal in mind. You want to make an adventure out of driving across North America and experiencing as much wildlife and as many remote regions as possible. Although the journey will start in Boston and end in Los Angeles, you want to be in wilderness as much as possible. The route that you want to take uses many back roads, goes over seldom-used mountain passes and even takes you off-road at times. The scenery will be spectacular! You want to get into areas rarely travelled to see wildlife in the most remote regions. There are festivals and events happening in the small towns that you will pass through for supplies, so you want to plan your timing to coincide with these events, if possible. But your main objective is to get off the beaten track and experience as much of the wildlife and out-of-the-way places as possible. The route you have planned for this journey will fulfill your personal objectives. The journey is analogous to a business process. Business processes, like journeys, are paths that must be followed in order to fulfill specific objectives.

When the extent and nature of your journey has been established, you will need to determine the practical requirements for your trip. You'll need a rugged vehicle. Features such as high clearance, 4x4, off-road tires, a towing winch, and extra capacity fuel tanks will be essential. Without the proper equipment, you'll be restricted to taking more frequently travelled routes. You have very specific expectations of what this vehicle must handle in order for your trip to be a success. These requirements come from knowing the route and conditions along the way. Without this knowledge, it's not possible to specify the right vehicle. If you had chosen the direct, highway route between Boston and Los Angeles, your vehicle choice would be totally different. It would be possible to drive your family sedan the whole way. But that would not achieve your objective. How much is the right vehicle going to cost? You may have to extend your budget or reduce your requirements once you start to price various vehicles and their options. This could affect the route you have planned. You may have to change parts of the trip to travel over less rugged areas. But at least you know what is required in the right vehicle.

The vehicle you take on this journey is analogous to the technology that supports a business process. All the planning needed to determine the route and the vehicle requirements is analogous to the project that results in the design for the business processes and the requirements for the enabling technologies. Your journey, however, is not about the vehicle; it's about the experiences you will encounter along the way. But if you don't have the right vehicle, you'll never be able to take the route that meets your particular objectives. The journey and the vehicle are inseparably linked—but don't confuse the journey with the vehicle.

What would happen if you were forced to use the family sedan for your trip? This would change everything, and the route planning would become a very different exercise. You'd size up the car and realize that it couldn't possibly survive the rugged terrain. Your journey would have to be different from what you had envisioned. When you look at the places you really want to go, the vehicle would keep reminding you that it won't be able to take you there. You would consider adding options and modifying its structure, but determine this would be too risky and expensive. You would have to compromise and plan an alternative route that would give you some wilderness experiences but more highway driving than you wanted. What a disappointment! Planning a journey around a specific vehicle would limit your ability to fully realize your objective.

The analogy of the journey and the vehicle is similar to business processes and enabling technologies. In the same way that you have a personal objective to reach and so develop a trip plan that will let you achieve it, in business you need to start first with your strategy and business objectives and conduct a business process design project to develop the business processes that will achieve them. As you design the processes, you will start to see the necessary technology requirements to successfully support the processes. Without the proper enabling technologies, your processes will never succeed, and you will not meet your objectives. Like the journey and the vehicle, the business processes and enabling technologies are inseparably linked. Without knowing what the processes look like, and without realizing what features are required to support them, how can you expect to select the right technologies?

What if you are in a situation where you've been told which technology you will have to use to support your business? Just as the route planning for the journey became a different exercise when you had to take the family sedan, your business process design will take a different approach depending on the prescribed technology. This is not an ideal way to start a major business change initiative, although sometimes executives do find themselves in this unfortunate position. Don't knowingly place yourself there if you have the opportunity to do things in the correct sequence: Design the business processes that can achieve your objectives, develop the features and requirements needed from the technology to support the processes, and then go out and select a particular make and model of technology. Make sure that your technology vehicle is capable of taking you on the journey that will achieve your business objectives.

This analogy can be stretched even further. Consider it when faced with the many trade-off situations involving business objectives, business processes, and enabling technologies.

Process Visualization and Business Change Initiatives

Process Visualization is about confidently starting a major business change initiative. In our fast-paced business environment with its drive for rapid technology innovation, executives are constantly challenged to consider new business models and change the way their organizations operate. With current business technology becoming more prolific and commonplace, and ever-changing market demands turning up the pressure, organizations need to find ways to successfully maintain, enhance, and build relationships. They need to provide value in their value chain, and they need to be recognized as being able to do it better than both their current competitors and new entrants to their market.

If you could easily explore how proposed business change initiatives would affect your business operations and relationships before being implemented, would this increase your chances of success? If you could see how business strategies, business practices, and technologies such as e-business solutions will work before you give your approval to invest significant resources, would this raise your confidence in making decisions? The new business models emerging from e-business applications challenge status-quo relationships and the position of industry participants. They are insistent that we examine how to conduct business from new perspectives. They point to areas where process steps can be reduced, and increased value can be delivered to customers. But just rushing in and embracing any new concept without fully understanding its impact is not the path to success. Going from the sales demonstration of a technology to implementation is a formula for disaster. There are plenty of technology implementations that fail to deliver on their promise to achieve solid business benefits. When they really fail and cause the business to suffer, they become news.

If you could get all the people with diverse views on the business and information technology sides of your organization to understand and pull in the same direction with confidence, do you think that the design of the new business concept and its enabling technology would have a better chance of being successfully implemented? Process Visualization gives people from all areas of expertise a common language as they start down the path to change their business practices and implement new supporting technologies. It gives them a forum to express their new ideas so that they are widely understood. Process Visualization provides the foundation for building a competent design team that is able to tackle business and technology issues. If first getting your business processes right and integrated before going on to the technology integration and implementation sounds like the correct order in which to do things, then Process Visualization is for you. Process Visualization encourages you to take the time at the start of your business change projects to ensure that everyone on the team and the executive are knowledgeable and buy into the design and technology. You should take the time up front to get it right because the costs to re-do it from a monetary, time, and credibility perspective are just too high.

An interesting phenomenon happened early in 2001 when the shine came off the technology sector. As the U.S. economy slowed, this sector experienced a recession and its equity markets tumbled. Technology started to be viewed differently. The new economy versus old economy viewpoint became less in vogue. There was a return to enduring values: profit, relationships, and customer service. The three-legged stool of people, process, and technology has returned to having three equally sized legs. Speed-to-market and a competitive edge are still the drivers that cause us to experiment and change. But there is a return to the realization that an innovative concept badly implemented will fail to deliver the anticipated benefits, but that same idea implemented well will achieve and sustain the benefits until it too is improved upon. Technology continues to be seen as a sector that will continue to grow and support our businesses in interesting ways. *Process Visualization* is about taking a balanced approach to implementing exciting new concepts so that your people, processes, and technologies will together make your organization succeed in tomorrow's markets.

PART ONE

Is Process
Visualization
for You?

The first part of this book deals with the what, where, and why of Process Visualization, Process Culture, and PeopleFlow.

Chapter 1 explains *what* it means when you employ the concepts of Process Visualization. An analogy to designing and testing a new car is used to show that visualization is a powerful design tool that could also be employed in business design. The chapter continues by listing the business situations *where* Process Visualization is most useful in developing integrated business process designs.

Chapter 2 If the benefits of Process Visualization are not compelling, then you will not be motivated to introduce it into your organization. This chapter outlines ways to look at the measurable and intangible benefits that you can expect from Process Visualization. It shows you *why* Process Visualization is of value to your organization.

Chapter 3 talks about Process Culture and provides an overview of this broad and much written about subject. This chapter examines the stages at which organizations find themselves as they strive to achieve the ideal of Process Culture. It demonstrates the contribution that Process Visualization can have on this process. In fact, with Process Visualization you can make a quantum leap.

Chapter 4 introduces PeopleFlow. This chapter explains *what it is* and *what it is not*. PeopleFlow is the toolkit that packages the concepts of Process Visualization. A case history explains how a major retailer used PeopleFlow to design new processes and system requirements to enhance their supply chain. It shows how executive approval was achieved for the business process design and how it proceeded to the implementation phase that involved a new Enterprise System, major modifications to their Warehouse Management System, and enhanced use of an Advanced Planning System.

CHAPTER ONE

ᏅᎧ

What Is Process Visualization?

What if you could visualize your business just like you watch a movie or a play? What if you could see how the people, processes, and technologies all work together in your business? What if you had a clear vision of how information, products and services, physical equipment, and money all flow through the processes and systems that define your business operations? If you could see what your people do and how technology supports them today, would it give you a better understanding of the need to change and improve your business practices and supporting technologies? Instead of imagining the possibilities offered by emerging technologies, what if you could see their impact on your business before you start to implement them? Sounds too much like fun and not work? It is playacting, but it's serious play, and it produces results. This is the essence of Process Visualization.

Process Visualization is about making change happen. In today's world of e-business, with its drive for rapid technology innovation, executives are constantly challenged to consider new business models and change the way their organizations operate. Process Visualization helps ensure that when change happens, everyone changes in the same direction. When you want or need to change, Process Visualization provides effective tools at the start of your implementation journey. It assists you to design, test, and approve your proposed business changes. Through Process Visualization you understand better how changes in strategies and policies will affect your relationships throughout your value chain. As a busy executive, it gives you the ability to be involved and play an effective role in the approval of new business ideas and proposed changes. When you can visualize how a new business model will successfully operate, you gain the confidence to invest in the people, processes, and technology required to make it happen. Process Visualization is a vital step in preparing your organization for a successful implementation project. Everyone comes away with a deeper understanding of both the business and technical integration requirements, and the issues that need to be addressed to make your implementation a success.

Visualization Is a Part of Our Everyday Lives

You have probably heard and said thoughts like these many times:

"When I was watching the movie, I really felt that I was there."

"I got an idea of what it was like back then and a good feeling about the lives that people used to lead."

"Now that I've seen the movie, I'd like to spend the time and read the book."

"The play really brought out the plight of the characters for me. I could feel their emotions and what they had to go through."

"The actors in the play made their characters come alive."

"There were some great ideas and thoughts expressed in the play. It made me want to find out more about the subject."

Many people prefer to see a movie than read a book, and almost no one reads the scripts of plays. They would rather see the play acted out for them in a theatre. Movies and plays make stories come alive for us. You can live lives and experience a different time and place in less than two hours and walk away with a lot to talk about. You can discuss the plot and form an opinion of the characters and their behaviour. You can decide how you might have done things differently or get insight into circumstances that you may never have thought of before. This is the impact that visualization can have on us—it can let us experience a great deal in a very short time.

Visualization is a strong part of gaining an understanding of any subject. But after watching a play or movie, many people become interested in knowing more than the actors were able to convey within the performance. Reading the book on which a play is based, after you've seen the performance, adds more depth to your experience and understanding.

Visualization Is Not Common in Business

You've probably never heard these thoughts expressed at work:

"That play really brought out how our policies can affect some of our customers."

"Now I understand why those people take so long to serve a single customer. Those actors were good at showing us the problems with our systems."

"I never really knew how important planning could be to our operations. Now that I've actually seen how it relates to the rest of our business, I understand why we need to get into Advanced Planning Systems."

"I'd heard a bit about this new Customer Relationship Management initiative that we're thinking about but I didn't see what it would do for us until I saw it being performed. Now I get it!"

"I always had the suspicion that we were not getting the right information out to the field in a timely manner. But the actors who performed how our information flows brought it home for me."

"I never laughed so hard. You should see how many things can go wrong when we process a customer order. The actors had a lot of fun bringing out our problems. But you know, we could all see ways to improve things."

"In the performance I saw what the new policies were supposed to do for us, but they just don't work for me yet. We need to rethink some of the exceptions, and then have our team act it out again."

Visualization Is Familiar Where New Products Are Designed and Prototyped

In product manufacturing companies, the activities of designing, prototyping, and testing all play a strong role. Whether it's for a new car, an airplane, a computer, or a space shuttle, the product's design and performance are critical in order to maintain and/or gain a competitive advantage in the marketplace. The activities of a product design cycle are embedded in a manufacturing company's culture because they require them to survive.

New car designs are today created in 3-D media that allows them to be visualized from all directions and in a number of interesting ways. The prototype model of a new car is put through its paces by simulating real-world tests. It's put into virtual wind tunnels and crashed into virtual walls. Watching and analyzing the results causes the team to rethink and improve their designs. Seeing the stress points, the crumpling of metal, and the actions inside the car of the dummies is important to fully understand the nature of an accident. Visualizing the experience of a crash test is as critical to understanding the new car's design strengths and performance as analyzing the data collected during the test.

A successful products company would not consider bringing a new product to market until it is sure that the design, prototype, and tests produce the results it is looking for. Visualizing how the product looks, understanding how it performs, and feeling confident in its safety are all key to the product's launch. Executives approve the launch of the production of a product when they are confident that the prototype not only looks great, but performs well. Everyone wants to know that they have produced a winner.

Why isn't this same approach applied to other aspects of business? Why not prototype your business processes and simulate them to visualize how they will stand up to real-world scenarios?

What Do We Mean by Process Visualization?

We have, so far, discussed two ideas: how visualization is used in plays and movies, and the value of visualization in new product design. Process Visualization brings together these two ideas. It uses the concept of actors performing in a play and combines it with the concept of prototyping and testing that takes place in designing a product.

In the same way that new products go through rigorous testing, business processes also need to be tested to prove that they can stand up to the stress and strain of their operating conditions. Just as a new product needs to be approved before you make the investment in production and marketing, a new or revised business process also needs executive approval before you make the investment in systems, technologies, and people. Why would you launch your business processes into action without putting them through the same kind of scrutiny that takes place in a product development environment?

What If. . .

What if you could visualize a business process just like you do a movie or a play? This is the cornerstone of Process Visualization. Wouldn't it enhance the experience of designing, testing, and approving business processes if you could see the processes in action? Since the new or revised business processes may be used to significantly change the way you conduct your business practices and interact with your customers and suppliers, it may be beneficial to know that they have been simulated and thoroughly tested so that they have shown they can stand up under stress. Before you invest in new technologies, you might like to be certain that they can actually run your own specific business processes, and not just someone else's.

Process Visualization brings simple and effective ways to let you see your business processes in action. This way of looking at process design can become embedded in your organization's culture. You can treat a business process design project like a new product design project. If you can effectively visualize your business processes—if you can see that they are integrated, if you are confident they will deliver your strategy to the marketplace, and if you understand how they will be supported by technologies—this could make a difference to the success of their implementation.

Business Process

Business process is a term with a broad meaning. The word "process" has come to mean more than just the activities and flows in a business. The term "business process" is commonly thought to contain many more business elements. Business process means the relationships that result between the following:

- business objectives, requirements, policies and rules, and best practices

- activities of people within your organization as well as external stakeholders (customers, customers' customers, suppliers, and service providers)

- flow of information, products and services, equipment, and money

- role and support provided by systems and other enabling technology; the features and functionality of these systems

- assumptions and accepted practices within your organization

Getting a Grasp on the Essential Elements

Process Visualization can provide you with the ability to grasp the essential elements and integration of your business processes. It's a satisfying feeling when you gain an understanding of any subject for the first time. A light bulb suddenly comes on! For this to happen you need to clearly see the integrated relationships between all the business elements that comprise a business process. This clarity allows you to see the impact of your proposed new policies and business practices on your customers and suppliers before they are even launched. Now you really know how things are working—or not. You understand the strengths and weaknesses of the process, and you can see how it can be improved. You can confidently manage and influence the process because it has come alive in your mind. It's like listening to a symphony orchestra, when you have the comprehension to discern the individual instruments, sense the tight relationship between the conductor and the musicians, and yet also appreciate the overall, integrated beauty of the music.

Process Visualization lets you understand in a totally new way how your business operates. It provides the big picture so that people with varied backgrounds, perhaps for the first time, understand the importance of integrated business processes. It stresses integration. It simulates how the internal parts of your business link together to form an integrated face to customers and suppliers. It portrays the role that your operations play in your industry's integrated value chain. By watching and listening to how manual and automated processes work, you understand where the value is in the touch points and relationships throughout the value chain and how you might act to change them and gain further competitive advantages.

Performing Your Business Processes

The heart of Process Visualization is the *performing* of your business processes. What would it take for you to be able to visualize a business process just like you do a play? The people in your organization must become the actors. They must develop a script that is the design of the new business processes. They will refine it by performing it amongst themselves. Finally, they will stage, for the executives and stakeholders, a performance that's very like a play.

The performance will tell the story of how your business processes and their enabling technologies will handle real-world scenarios. It should tell how information flows will support the activities of the process, and how people will work and interact with each other and with the supporting systems. The story will involve the relationships with your customers and suppliers. And like all good plots, the play will deal with problems, issues, and hurdles that the characters must overcome. It will strive to leave the audience with a satisfying ending! A successful ending is one where your business processes are robust, where they can stand up to the pressured situations that they will likely encounter, where your customers understand and like what the enhanced new relationship does for them, and where it is demonstrated that the processes can be enabled with proven technologies.

How are the actors going to accomplish the challenge of letting you experience the inner workings of your business? Unfortunately, we can't climb into a capsule and miniaturize ourselves like the man in the movie, "Fantastic Voyage," who travelled through the human body. Business processes are not objects that can be modelled in 3-D, so we can't fly through them like we can through models of buildings.

But the sense of travelling *through* the inner workings of a business process design needs to be brought to life. A business process, as we have defined it, consists of many business elements. It has manual activities, automated activities, and information flows that occur within computer systems, products moving on vehicles, decisions being made by both people and systems, and interactions between people and systems. The activities of people and the flow of products are relatively easy to perform and bring to life. Stage props such as boxes of product, bar-coded labels, laser pens acting as scanners, and a wagon substituting for a truck, can be used to enhance the effect of the movement of the physical product through its supply chain. But we need to be in that special capsule that can be injected into and travel through the technologies that enable our business processes.

Actors need to take on the roles of the automated activities and information flows that happen inside systems and technologies. The flow of information from people into systems, back out for people to use and change, and back in to be retained until required again needs to be portrayed in a way that clearly shows the uses of information flows and relationships between technology and people. Information flow is the key that drives the need for technology support in the first place. Physical products don't flow inside a computer system. It's the information *about* the physical product that flows through a system. Information is also created in the system by calculating and planning each time a product moves. This plan is then presented to a person for review, modification, and approval. To fully understand how physical products move in a supply chain, you must understand the information flows that plan and control their movements. For instance, to understand the supply chain concept of replacing inventory with information, you need to see how timely information is essential and how it is used to forecast customer demand, calculate inventory levels, and plan product movements before they are executed. Information use, flow, and timeliness are all key elements that need to be conveyed in a manner that will hold your attention. If you can be like the person in the capsule and travel through the inner workings of a system, experiencing how information supports your business processes, then you will come away with a deeper understanding of how your business processes will work and how technologies are essential to support them.

Sometimes people ask: "Why go through all the work to perform the business process; why not just see a demonstration of the system?" The answer is simple: You can never see what's happening behind the computer screen. In a flash, information can be retrieved, calculations can be done, and the screen displays all the information you supposedly need. It's impressive, but did you understand what just happened? Do you know why you need this screen of information in front of you and what it took to get it? Using a single screen to flash information is a myopic approach that seldom leads to understanding and rarely builds confidence in executives. Will a simple demonstration really convince you that the entire system will work in your organization and should be implemented right now? No executive should approve technology purchases and implementations of major business change initiatives just because they have seen an impressive system demonstration.

Participative Theatre as Part of the Design Process

You can use the idea of performing business processes to accomplish a number of tasks in a design process. Design is an iterative process, and performing can effectively be used throughout its various steps. Recall the product design cycle where a new product has to go through a cycle of design, testing, redesign, further tests, initial attempt at approval, perhaps redesign, confirmation tests, and eventually final approval. Designers use high-tech prototypes or simple physical models to assist them in all the steps of designing the product and simulating its operating conditions. The same can be true when designing your business processes. They should be put through the same rigorous process. Your business processes can be performed at each step along the iterative design path. By going through iterations of the design cycle objectively and responding to the refined design with constructive criticism, you can help the business processes move towards their optimum design and achieve the organization's business objectives.

How to Use Participative Theatre Along the Iterative Path of Designing Business Processes

Design

At the start of the design step:
The design team takes the initial design ideas that they have rapidly developed by considering only the major requirements and immediately starts to use performing to further develop their process design.

Throughout the design step:
New ideas and scenarios are thought of that need to be considered. The design team formulates how they should work and then immediately performs them so that everyone on the team can see the new idea in action.

How to Use Participative Theatre Along the Iterative Path of Designing Business Processes (*continued*)

Test

More simulations of various business scenarios that will be encountered need to be formulated and then tested. The design team performs the list of scenarios. Often the executive sponsor and some key stakeholders will see the design at this early stage in order to offer guidance. Performing the scenarios is the simulation test that lets everyone see how the processes stand up to actual business scenarios. Most often there are parts of the process that need to go through another iteration to redesign and fine-tune aspects of the design.

Initial Approval

The initial approval step gets more people involved in understanding the proposed new business process design. This is where more of the executive and stakeholders become involved in the design steps. The design team performs a few key scenarios that best depict the new design and its robustness in various business conditions. The executives use this opportunity to quickly understand the essence of the design. They ask questions, give their advice, and make suggestions for improvements. It is not unusual to ask the team to go back to refine or redesign aspects of the process.

Redesign and Test

New and changed directives, refined requirements, further ideas, and scenarios will arise from the initial approval step in an iterative design process. The team will reconsider and rework the processes to include all these factors in the final design. They formulate how the new ideas should work, and then perform them so that everyone on the team can see the new idea in action and test that the integrated design still holds together.

Final Approval

This is usually a shorter performance of the business processes and may include only those sections of the design that the executive sent the design team back to redesign. Final approval does not mean this is the last time the executive can see and approve the direction of the business change initiative. It means that the design is ready to go into the next phase of the program that involves the enabling technologies.

Performing to Educate and Market

You need to educate and in some cases market the newly designed business processes to stakeholders and people affected by the proposed changes. Stakeholders and others affected by the proposed changes will need to be convinced of the benefits to them of change. Performing key business scenarios is a good way to educate them and gain buy-in for the changes that will soon occur. Watching a performance of the proposed new design will help to alleviate the fear of the unknown that often exists for those not directly involved in the project. Performing is also a good way to involve your customers and suppliers and gain acceptance from them right up front. Now is a good time to show external stakeholders what changes are coming and how they will benefit from them.

Process Documentation

Process Visualization relies on proper documentation. In order to produce a play, the actors, director, and production crew all rely on a script. They breathe life into the story through their skills at interpreting the written word. They transform a written document into an interesting experience by making the characters and plot come alive for us. In a play, the script is all that physically remains after the curtain comes down at the end. Without the existence of a script, there would be no record.

Business processes also need to be documented. Their script needs to be developed as the design progresses. The characteristics of a business process require various ways to capture the design in a meaningful manner. The activities, information flows, requirements, rules, and policies must be documented so that they are easy to understand. When the performance is over, you will continue to use and rely on a well-organized, easy-to-follow style of business process documentation.

Where Is Process Visualization Used?

There are two factors that cause organizations to launch business change initiatives: change driven by technology and change driven by business events.

Change Driven by Technology

You can use Process Visualization in change initiatives driven by technology. Technology is ubiquitous in supporting business activities. Emerging technologies fuel the drive for gaining a competitive advantage. The relationship between business processes and the systems and technologies that enable the processes is so close that it's impossible to deal with one without the other. Technology is often the trigger that makes organizations consider a major change initiative. When technology drives the change, business processes and people need to respond to ensure that all three are aligned. Table 1.1 shows situations where technology can be the trigger for change.

TABLE 1.1: Scenarios Where Technology Is the Trigger for Change

Your organization wants to explore new e-business concepts.	**The technology has already been purchased.**
You want to explore technologies involving the Internet, such as e-commerce (exchanges and auctions), m-commerce (mobile and wireless), and c-commerce (collaboration). If these strategies appear beneficial, you will adopt them and implement the supporting technology. How will the new technology influence your processes and people? All three elements must be aligned to ensure you realize the benefits.	Now the task falls to you to implement it successfully! Even though it was not your choice, the challenge is to go forward and make it a success. If the "fit" isn't what you expected, how will you explore how processes can effectively be changed to accommodate the system without negatively impacting the business? How do you recognize when some modifications are necessary?

TABLE 1.1: Scenarios Where Technology Is the Trigger for Change (*continued*)

Packaged software offers a popular approach for implementing new concepts.	**You have already implemented a premier business system, but you feel your organization is not fully benefiting from the strengths of the technology.**
Advanced Planning Systems (APS) and Customer Relationship Management (CRM) are two currently popular supply chain concepts that organizations are buying and implementing. Enterprise Systems (ES), or Enterprise Resource Planning (ERP) systems, are still being purchased, implemented, and upgraded. How will the concepts and suggested best practices offered by the software affect your business processes and people? How will you select and then implement the new system?	Perhaps your concern is over your ES (such as SAP, JD Edwards, Oracle). Or maybe your APS (such as i2 Technologies or Manugistics) is not increasing service levels. Is it possible your CRM system (such as Siebel, Pivotal, or Saratoga) is not creating the value with your customers that you envisioned? Is it the system's functionality, your people's understanding, or your processes that need to be re-aligned?

Change Driven by Business Events

Change initiatives driven by business events can also benefit from Process Visualization. Change does not just wait for a new technology solution to appear before forcing organizations to be more competitive. Change drivers within your industry and the marketplace can cause you to look at how people, process, and technology might be changed to enhance your competitive position. Sometimes events inside your organization make you examine change initiatives. Technology, business processes, and people all need to respond to change driven by business events. Table 1.2 shows situations where business events trigger change initiatives.

TABLE 1.2: Scenarios Where Business Events Are the Trigger for Change

Customers and suppliers are pushing you.	**You are working through a merger.**
Your external stakeholders want to form tighter relationships with you. Suppliers want to get further than your receiving dock with their relationship. Customers want you to take more responsibility in their organizations for your products and services. A strong mutual trust is needed to make the proposed partnerships work. The concepts sound interesting to you, but do you understand how it will all work? How will the new relationship benefit your organization?	Both organizations have their own systems and business processes, but you need to put the organizations together. What are the strengths and weaknesses of the systems and processes that are coming together? How do you choose between them or take the best of both worlds and make it work?
You are about to outsource part of your operations.	**Continuous improvement programs give you benefits of ongoing incremental changes.**
It could be your supply chain operations, customer service and accounts receivable, or procurement and payables that you are going to outsource. You need to ensure that all the processes affecting customers and suppliers continue to operate in a seamless manner. How will you ensure that the people, processes, and technologies from both organizations align to enhance service to customers?	You want to continuously refine your processes and systems and receive the benefits from ongoing incremental change by using Process Visualization. Using it on a continuous basis can ensure that your people are prepared when a major change initiative occurs.

TABLE 1.2: Scenarios Where Business Events Are the Trigger for Change (*continued*)

The explosive growth in your organization is overwhelming your resources.	You need to look at the effectiveness of your processes, people, and supporting technology.
Before your high level of customer service starts to fail, you need to relieve the pressure on the organization. Your best people are stretched. But what needs to be fixed? Does the answer lie in more people, improved business processes, or better technology support?	Things seem out of line; your expense-to-sales ratio looks high. You may not want to call it re-engineering, because of the connotations of the term. But, you need to do something that objectively investigates where the problem lies.

Don't Be Put Off by Re-engineering Failures

Business Process Re-engineering (BPR) failures have tarnished the reputation of the business process approach. People tend to shy away from saying the word "re-engineering." BPR has fallen out of favour because of the connotations of downsizing and right-sizing. It is commonly felt that the focus of re-engineering is to reduce costs by reducing headcount.

But business processes have not gone away. Companies that want to bring in a new business model driven by e-business technologies will be doing things differently in the future. They will be altering aspects of their relationship with customers and suppliers. Because of the dominant role that technology plays in these change initiatives, it's especially important that organizations remember to include their business processes and people in the implementation. With Process Visualization there is a better way to approach your business processes when changes are about to happen.

Do not shy away from business processes because of one word in the abbreviation BPR. Technology will not automatically implement itself and run your organization's processes the way you envision. Keep focused on the positive aspects of processes and keep promoting their importance in your organization. Process Visualization can help you in your efforts to improve and change your business processes, without the connotations associated with re-engineering. Do not be put off by the failure of re-engineering.

Why Use Process Visualization?

Process Visualization: Tangible and Intangible Benefits

The first chapter introduced the *what* of Process Visualization. Now, it's time to consider the *why*. Why should you consider using it—what's in it for you and your organization? Executives first want to hear the answer to *why* in monetary terms. How much will they save if they adopt Process Visualization? What's the return? These are fair questions. This chapter begins by explaining where measurable savings can be realized. Then, it moves on to examine the intangible benefits.

The Tangible Benefits of Process Visualization

The most significant tangible benefit of using Process Visualization is cost avoidance through implementing the initiative right—the first time. The cost of failure, in terms of time, money, and credibility, can be significant. Failures are often followed by further rounds of implementation projects that can cause considerable stress on budgets. Even with an implementation that does not fail, but keeps dragging on because of all the problems and issues that cause rework to happen, the costs continue to mount and the time to realize business benefits extends further out into the future. Process Visualization, used at the start of your change initiative, can help you to avoid these unexpected costs. Even before you start your implementation you can have a direct impact on your expenses by lowering your reliance on external consulting resources. Your own people can confidently conduct more of the process design work themselves. Process Visualization can make your cost/benefit and return on investment analysis look better as you are preparing your project justifications.

Save Time, Money, and Credibility

How much does it cost you when failure in a technology implementation program leads to business failure? How much time, money, and credibility are lost when a technology fails to enable the business processes and this leads to the business failing to deliver its results? You can use Process Visualization to help avoid a significant technology implementation disaster that could result in your business faltering and suffering while the damage is repaired. If you can get the business processes right at the start of the project, you increase your chances of successfully implementing the systems and realizing the business benefits that the technology has to offer. Ignore the business processes and you risk a disaster.

When a major multi-national organization runs into problems with a technology implementation, especially one involving e-business, it becomes news. You can find enough of these stories in the media to realize that failure isn't just a chance occurrence. The dollar amounts in these stories are often quite large. Disasters happen and you want to avoid them. You don't want to be the next CEO trying to justify your organization's innocence in a sad business affair.

Take the recent case of Nike and its implementation of i2 Technologies (Advanced Planning System), SAP (Enterprise System), and Siebel (Customer Relationship Management). Nike reported a quarterly sales shortfall of over $100 million and blamed the problem on the i2 planning system for creating serious inventory problems. Nike's CEO Philip Knight is reported by the Internet Week Web site (see Reference article indicated by [1]) to have said, "This is what we get for our $400 million?" Nike and i2 blamed each other. When you read more about the story and look at comments about how to avoid a similar disaster, a few common themes emerge. One that comes to the forefront is the importance of getting the business process right up front. After an implementation disaster makes the news, everyone asks: Who took the time to understand the business processes; were there well-thought-out business rules to drive the planning systems; and was the executive involved in policy formulation?

In any disaster you can ask the same questions of people in the organization, the software vendor, and the systems integrator and get different answers and perspectives on what went wrong. But one thing that everyone will agree on is this:

"If you can get the business processes 'right' at the start of the project, you increase your chances of successfully implementing the systems and realizing the business benefits that the functionality of the technology has to offer. Ignore the business processes and you risk a disaster."

Business processes, along with all their component parts, are what the system has to emulate and support. If you can't describe them, how can you expect the system to be configured to enable them? How will you know if the functionality in the software won't support your processes and therefore will need to be modified? Without clear specifications and an understanding on everyone's part about how the team envisions the business working, it is no surprise that finger pointing happens from all sides in the battle for credibility.

There are other examples apart from Nike that you can read about if you need to be convinced further (see Reference articles indicated by [2]). Major corporations in the news with well-publicized problems and failures dealing with ERP system implementations include FoxMeyer Drug Corporation, Hershey Foods, Mobil Europe, Whirlpool, and W.L. Gore and Associates. It's evident that disasters impose a high cost on everyone involved. Can you calculate the cost to your organization and to you personally if your business were to falter due to a technology's failure to support your business processes? Could it be large enough for you to be caught in the evening's headlines?

Process Visualization gets your business processes ready to start the technology implementation phase. Focusing on your business processes as the first step in a business change initiative can reduce the risk of a catastrophe down the road.

Lower Your Reliance on Consulting Resources

Process Visualization is about being self-sufficient. It's about building trust and confidence in the ability of your people to design and implement business processes. By lessening your dependency and reliance on consulting resources, you can reduce costs dramatically on your business process projects. You will only need to use consulting resources for the skills that you don't have in-house. Knowing how to design and test business processes is a skill your teams can learn. In fact, they can become very proficient at it. They may, in fact, become better at it than the consultants!

There's a well-known saying: "Give a community food, and you feed them for a day; teach them how to grow their food, and you feed them for a lifetime." By adapting this wisdom to business you get the saying: "Give an organization a consultant, and you support the organization for one project; teach the people in an organization how to do it themselves, and you support them for a lifetime of change." There is no question that it's possible to drastically reduce the use of consulting resources when you have the confidence to do the work yourself. A large organization's annual consulting expenses can approach, and often exceed, $1 million on work that helps to formulate business models, to design business processes, to implement new technologies, to promote stakeholder buy-in, and to facilitate change management. If this cost were reduced by even a small percentage by adopting Process Visualization, it would generate significant savings.

Achieve Further Savings by Avoiding Common Pitfalls

There are further monetary savings to be achieved by avoiding the pitfalls that commonly occur during and after technology implementation projects. Although these are not the major disasters discussed earlier, they are the ones that cause death-by-a-thousand-cuts. When this syndrome creeps in, it consumes further resources and valuable time to fix the problems. Some organizations never seem to be able to escape this state. Which pitfalls have happened to you and how much does it cost each time they happen?

How much do design "misses" cost?

What does it cost to go back and make design changes after you've passed the design phase of the project? Every time a change is made it causes a chain reaction of activities that need to be redone. The further along in the project that they are discovered, the more steps there are that need to be fixed. Think of all the steps that happen in an implementation and what it takes to redo a tiny part of each one over again. How much does this cost in terms of money and lost time? How long are you delayed from realizing the benefits because the implementation and rework drag on?

What does it cost to redo parts of a system implementation after you realize that it was only a technical implementation and did not focus on business processes?

This is the worst-case scenario of the point discussed above. You wanted a quick implementation and you achieved it. But, now you realize that the stopwatch is still ticking because you have not achieved any real business benefits. People have been trained on the system's functionality but not on how the business processes and policies are supposed to work. Everyone is complaining about the failure of the system to support their business activities, but the real failure was in the design of the processes and in the education of the people. Success starts when you reap the business benefits, not when you throw the new system's switch to the "live" position. You will find yourself still running the same race instead of moving on to the next opportunity.

How much does it cost to modify the software package because you rushed into an implementation without first knowing how to critically examine business processes from end to end and how to look for the potential to re-align them?

How much have you lost in the ability to easily move to the next release of the system? Once you have the millstone of modifications around your neck, you keep paying for them from release to release. Modifications are not a one-time cost. Each time you want to advance with your system vendor to the next release, you pay to take them along. Total cost = [one-time modification costs] + [cost to take modifications to next release × the number of release upgrades over the lifetime of the software]. If you are doing this calculation for your Enterprise Resource Planning (ERP) system, you can expect to keep it for five to 10 years, and upgrade two to five times in that period. You probably can't avoid making some modifications, especially to ERP packages. But you can reduce the number of modifications if you spend the time to critically examine your processes and the way the package can be configured to support various approaches to the process.

How much does it cost when key stakeholders don't buy-in?

Have you experienced resistance from customers, suppliers, and employees who constantly fight the changes that you have recently implemented? Did you include these key stakeholders early on in the design process or just spring the changes on them when you were ready to launch? Often it is not *what* you change, but *how* you change that makes all the difference. Your policies and business rules are reflected in the value propositions to your customers and suppliers. These are all contained and enabled by the newly implemented system. What does it cost when people start to work around the system and execute their own ideas about how the business rules and policies should operate? Buy-in and understanding of how the value propositions are delivered by the End-to-End processes can help to achieve acceptance and generate expected benefits.

The Intangible Benefits of Process Visualization

Let's look at some of the intangible benefits that Process Visualization can achieve. The list is headed by confidence because it's key to a successful launch of the implementation phase of a business change initiative. An environment for innovation is created in your organization when you use Process Visualization. It makes conflict resolution easier and lets you reach consensus, conclusions, and decisions faster. Creativity and fun are also a part of this environment. Clearly defined techniques and standards focus the team's work to produce designs that are tested for business integration. Process Visualization can provide you with insights about your current business and your proposed changes.

Build Confidence in Your Ability to Realize Business Benefits

Confidence builds on itself when Process Visualization is involved in a design project. Diagram 2.1 shows how Process Visualization is a key contributor to building confidence in an organization from the very start of the program. Confidence in the design needs to be there before the implementation phase begins.

Confidence building starts with the design team.

Your business process design team needs to fully understand that Process Visualization can effectively guide them through the steps of developing, simulating, and testing business processes. The goal of successfully implementing the new design is increased significantly when the entire team understands and follows the concepts of Process Visualization. Designing business processes is not necessarily a natural talent, nor does anyone have it just because he or she has been doing a job for a number of years. Even if you have chosen good people, it doesn't mean they can automatically express in process terminology what they do every day in their job. A common language and the ways to think about process design can easily be learned. The team needs to learn the techniques and tools that will be needed for the task ahead. Team members need to gain confidence in their ability to operate as an effective design group. Training and certification at the outset, before they even look at your current business processes, give individuals a tremendous sense of clarity and direction. In Part

II, Process Thinking goes into further details about the techniques and tools in the PeopleFlow toolkit. Refer to Appendix A, page 161, for more information on team training and certification. When people have the right tools and know what is expected of them, they can confidently tackle the task at hand. After gaining an understanding of Process Visualization, the team will feel they can get right into the design work. The team gains confidence in its own ability to deliver an innovative design that can be implemented.

The team's confidence and knowledge starts to build trust and confidence among the executive.

A well-selected team that has been trained and certified sends strong signals to the organization. Everyone expects a lot from the team's efforts. It takes a while for a design team to find its stride, but the results will soon start to appear. The executives most closely impacted by the project and the executive sponsor soon start to see the team's ability to resolve major design issues and overcome hurdles. The team learns when to call for help and when they need to pass policy and business rule issues on to the executive to resolve. The ability of the team to work closely with the executive and hand off situations for them to resolve with policy and rule definitions conveys that your design process is working well. Executive members gain trust in the process and in the team. As the team starts to unfold the design, executive members informally sit in on

Diagram 2.1   Confidence building is a chain reaction.

Confidence needs to be built and sustained during a major technology implementation program. Here's how Process Visualization can build confidence from the very beginning of a project.

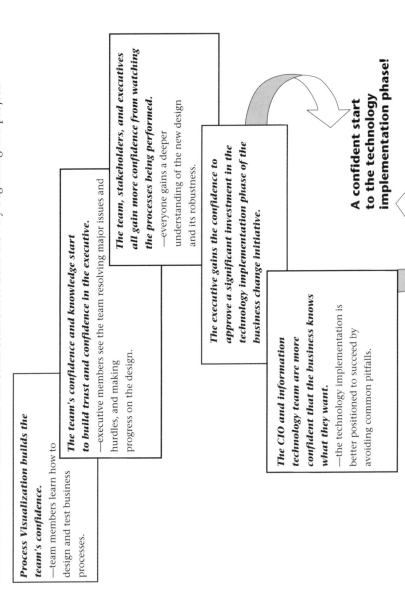

Process Visualization builds the team's confidence.
—team members learn how to design and test business processes.

The team's confidence and knowledge start to build trust and confidence in the executive.
—executive members see the team resolving major issues and hurdles, and making progress on the design.

The team, stakeholders, and executives all gain more confidence from watching the processes being performed.
—everyone gains a deeper understanding of the new design and its robustness.

The executive gains the confidence to approve a significant investment in the technology implementation phase of the business change initiative.

The CIO and information technology team are more confident that the business knows what they want.
—the technology implementation is better positioned to succeed by avoiding common pitfalls.

A confident start to the technology implementation phase!

design performance sessions; everyone's sense of achievement and confidence grows.

The team, stakeholders, and executives gain more confidence when they watch the processes being performed.

Everyone involved in approving the processes attends the process performance sessions. Executives and stakeholders gain a deeper understanding of the new design and its robustness. The team also learns from these sessions. The rework that they're given to do, and the discussions around what looks right and what doesn't, is an education for everyone. The confidence level of all participants rises as the design starts to firm up. At the final approval performance there's a high level of confidence that the design can work, can be implemented, and can deliver the desired business benefits.

Confidence in the process design leads to approval of the investment to proceed into the implementation phase.

As an executive, and as a member of the steering committee, your role is to approve and monitor the funding for business change initiatives. You need to have confidence that the implementation can be a success and that the expected business benefits are achievable. The investment in technology implementation can be significant. Shareholder value needs to be realized. Executives usually display confidence in the business process design when they see that it's possible to achieve the expected business benefits. It's important to have confidence instilled in the executive before they fully commit to the implementation phase, because it's here that the risks and major expenditures start to happen. Confidence, now, is important because a realistic executive knows that even with the right design, the journey through a technology implementation is not necessarily an easy one to make.

The CIO and information technology team are more confident that the business knows what they want.

Your CIO and IT team know the pitfalls that await them as they move into the technology implementation phase. They need to feel confident that they can successfully deliver a support system that will achieve the expected business benefits. This group, more than anyone, knows that they can fail dramatically when there is not a clear definition of the business requirements, business rules, policies, and processes. Today, technology is configured as much as it is built. Without defined business components, it's difficult to configure the settings in the software solution so that it will properly enable the business. The answers don't need to be carved in stone at this stage because there will still be options to explore. When the CIO and IT team have confidence that the business knows what it wants, it's a tremendous boost to them as they begin the technology phase of the change initiative.

Make Conflict Resolution Easier

Process Visualization creates a forum that allows sensitive issues and areas of high conflict to be resolved with a positive outcome.

You will always find differing opinions on how a business currently works, but these differences are usually easy to resolve. When it comes to designing new business processes and deciding how your business should and needs to work, disagreements can become more emotional. There are often camps formed around different perspectives, each with their heels firmly dug in on issues. Resolving these conflicting viewpoints in a way that allows everyone to reach agreement on controversial design issues is critical to the success of the design. If conflicts are not resolved, the new design may not make it to approval for implementation. Leaving conflict unresolved is a formula for disaster when the system goes live. I think that businesses can create a powerful competitive advantage that's hard to beat when they can resolve their own internal conflicts.

Process Visualization uses the idea of Participative Theatre to provide a forum for the resolution of conflicts and for the softening of positions taken on issues. Throughout performances, areas of conflict quickly surface. Process Visualization encourages those with opposing viewpoints to conduct their debate as a critique of the play. The simple technique of performing the processes, and acting the scenarios out with the problems and issues front and centre on the stage, creates an atmosphere where tensions and emotions are aimed at the play, not at individuals. It allows people to vent their frustrations and argue their position without becoming personal. All members of the audience are in essence working together in trying to rewrite the play the way they think the plot should unfold. The performance can demonstrate the strengths and weaknesses of the opposing positions, and it gives all sides a chance to see what really appears to work best for their business. In the end, maybe they reach a compromise, or maybe one side sees the error in their thinking, but in either case, Process Visualization provides a forum in which to resolve conflicts. This forum allows people to save face and find a solution that everyone can agree to work with as they go forward with the new process design.

Reach Consensus, Conclusions, and Decisions Faster—and Maintain the Quality of the Design

It's not only the methodology that determines the pace of the implementation. The speed at which executives make decisions is a major factor in expanding or contracting the timeline of a design project and an implementation. Failure to reach a consensus on business policies and rules in a timely manner can slow a design project down to a snail's pace. What can the team work on when so much is still hanging in the air? How can they design processes when they don't have the basic requirements and business rules? Executives need to reach conclusions fast if they want the term "rapid" to apply to their implementation. What can help you confidently make decisions in a timely manner to keep the project moving?

The design team faces a similar dilemma. They also need to reach consensus on issues, make decisions, and bring debate to a conclusion as quickly as possible. At the same time, they are charged with producing a quality design. The design process creates numerous trade-offs and decisions that need to be considered and resolved along the way to keep the project moving. If the team does not work efficiently during their design project, benefits will take longer to achieve. But, if they don't produce a quality design, few, if any, benefits will ever be achieved. The trade-off between speed and quality is a common one in business process designs and technology implementations. Without quality, speed really means nothing.

Through the performing of the processes, both the team members and the executives gain the ability to quickly and easily grasp the design, the issues, and the options for making decisions. When decisions have to be made, people can make them with more confidence. Decisions are made faster when people have more insight into the impact and resulting effects of their choice. Process Visualization can help you confidently make decisions faster.

Reach the True Milestone Faster

You can reach the true milestone faster—a realization of the business benefits. Technology vendors and systems integrators claim that their implementation methodology produces rapid results. Every executive wants to achieve a successful implementation as quickly as possible. This speed should result in a lower cost and a faster realization of the business benefits.

Make sure you are measuring your implementation to the right milestone. You are deceiving yourself if you think that the rapid implementation methodology means a race that's only timed to where you turn the system on live for a small pilot. You really need to measure the time to the point where you have rolled out and implemented the technology, and have started to realize the anticipated benefits. By measuring to this true milestone, you can assess the trade-off between speed and quality. Be careful of the claims that others make about the word "rapid." You need to measure yourself to the true finish line, not to just one of the many milestones along the way.

Process Visualization will get you more successfully to the finish line, but it makes no claim to being rapid. If you follow the concepts of Process Visualization, it may seem like you are getting off to a slower start. The business process design will no doubt take more time than a cursory design or a quick plunge straight into the technology. But if your objective is to produce a quality design that can be used to select and implement the technology, then the concepts in Process Visualization can benefit you. Process Visualization will get you to the true milestone faster.

Start Technology Integration Work Knowing That the Business Processes Are Integrated

If you can start your technology implementation knowing that the business processes are integrated, then you have accomplished a significant feat whose benefits everyone will continue to feel throughout the change initiative. Integrated business processes give your technology implementation the confidence to proceed with the technology integration issues.

When organizations implement new technologies to support their business change initiatives, they are more than likely dealing with a number of best-of-breed systems that need to be integrated. The task of a system integrator, or your internal IT group, is to take these various systems and link them so that information flows seamlessly through them to users across your organization. From deciding on a common definition for the information elements in the database to linking the software on different hardware platforms together, the technical challenge is daunting. Knowing that the business processes have been thoroughly designed and that the major information elements have also been defined and agreed to allows the technology team to confidently proceed with their work. Moving forward with an integrated business process design is a significant benefit.

Take, for example, the common case in a supply chain initiative of integrating your customer order processing system with a Customer Relationship Management (CRM) system, a Warehouse Management System (WMS), a Transportation Management System (TMS), an Advanced Planning System (APS), and a performance measurement system. What does the simple term "due date" on the customer order mean to you and to each of the systems? Is it the date the order is due to be shipped or the date it is due at the customer's dock? What about all the other terms that define the timeline of events and lead times during the flow of the customer order? If these definitions are not matched perfectly throughout the integrated systems and over different databases, then you have a serious problem that could lead to service level and inventory performance issues. If the people using the systems don't use the same definitions and the various systems use the information differently in their processing and calculations, then you do not have business integration. It's relatively simple to define and align all the terms so that they have a common meaning throughout your organization and inside the technologies. This simple example stresses the point that having your information flows integrated across all business processes before going on to tackle the technical integration allows your technology team to focus on their own issues. Technical integration work presents enough of a challenge without having to cycle back to resolve basic business integration issues.

Develop Documentation and Treat It as Intellectual Property

Treat your business process designs as you would any other intellectual property held by your organization. To be a valuable asset, process designs must be documented so that people who are not involved in their creation can easily access and understand them. Consistency is key when creating business process documentation. The people in your information technology group, no doubt, use a common methodology to document their system designs. Why shouldn't the business people in your organization do the same? The topic of business process documentation is probably not high on your list of priorities, but consider it from the intellectual-property perspective.

Process Visualization promotes business process documentation as an important foundation to communicating the design to others. It gives the design team a common language in which to discuss issues facing business processes. The team uses the simple building-block approach offered by Process Visualization to effectively explain current processes and to design new ones.

Don't think that all process documentation has the same merits. Just producing a single process chart using the standard symbols as defined in a drawing package does not produce sufficient business process documentation. You need to produce a set of documentation that will be accepted and used throughout your organization. You need to have well-documented processes so that the technology team has a solid foundation on which to take the next step and start their technology implementation work.

You will benefit from using a standard way to document all your business process projects whether your organization is designing new processes or improving current ones. Process Visualization has created standards for business process documentation that result in consistency and completeness. Your business process designs are an important asset of your organization. Make sure they are captured in a way that preserves their value.

Support Knowledge Management

Process Visualization supports knowledge management in its search for better ways to generate, retain, and share intellectual capital within organizations. Knowledge management is a relatively young field of study. It searches for ways to best generate, retain, and share knowledge within and between organizations. It examines why one system or business model works so well in one organization but fails in another. It looks at how and why one organization uses the same knowledge more effectively than its competitors. It tries to find knowledge management systems that work best in different types of organizations. And it explores how information technology can most effectively be used to retain and share knowledge. Knowledge management is concerned with how current knowledge is used and how new ideas are proposed to be used. This is exactly what Process Visualization offers to organizations in their business change initiatives.

Process Visualization is a small part of the much larger field of knowledge management. The simple concepts presented here can benefit those organizations that are interested in pursuing better ways to manage knowledge, just as they would other corporate assets. Process Visualization can form a part of your knowledge management tactics.

Compress the Strategy-to-Execution Cycle

You probably realize that there can be a significant lag between formulating a new business strategy and seeing it working and generating expected benefits. Your strategy could be to implement a business model that will dramatically change the way you do things today. For instance, a new e-business strategy and its business model could considerably modify the way in which you transact business with your customers and suppliers. Your role, and those of your customers and suppliers, would alter dramatically. How will you be sure that the business model being developed to support the strategy will match your expectations?

Prototyping and simulating the new business model is the answer to shrinking the strategy-to-execution cycle; this lets you get a glimpse of what the future will look like. The ability to experience a simulation of the concept before it's executed is the key to compressing the cycle.

Achieving an end result that the executive envisions is often a difficult goal to reach. Too often along the way the direction shifts because of what the software offers, or what IT wants, or what a business team leader wants. Many small shifts throughout the projects that make up the change initiative can lead, in the end, to a result that is not what the executive want to implement.

Process Visualization is all about prototyping and simulating your new business model so that you experience it sooner than if you had waited for the implementation to be completed. When different scenarios are performed, you will see much sooner in the cycle what to expect when you go live with a new business model. One of the intangible benefits of Process Visualization is this compression of time, the result of simulating how the strategy is going to be executed. If you see a gap between your strategy and how your design team thinks it should be executed, you have the opportunity to make the changes and adjust expectations—before implementation.

Create an Environment for Innovation

The people that you have chosen for your business process design team want to show that they can develop new and innovative business solutions to give their organization a competitive advantage in the marketplace. They have been chosen to participate in your major business change initiative because of their skills. These people are, for the most part, creative and full of new ideas. They know what is happening today with the current business processes, and many have kept up with the latest developments in your industry. What kind of environment are you going to provide for them so that they can succeed?

Process Visualization offers an environment that encourages innovation and creativity. It facilitates an atmosphere where all team members can participate and express their ideas. During the performing of the business process flows, all team members participate and have roles to play. At the same time, they are their own audience and critic. The performing style of Process Visualization creates an environment quite different from the traditional design session in which a few overbearing personalities often try to dominate with their ideas.

Process Visualization promotes improvisation. When the team is designing and performing business processes, new ideas inevitably come out of these sessions. "What if?" is heard a lot as the team tries out new ideas and thinks through the issues and design concerns that naturally surface when the processes are performed. Experimentation leads to innovative business solutions, and this is encouraged. The fact that the team speaks a common language helps them to formulate and express their new ideas to each other. The concepts within Process Visualization create a design environment that's very different from more traditional approaches and brings out the best in your people as they work to make the design project a success.

Enjoy the Fun and Laughter—They Produce Results

People on the design team have fun acting out the various roles in a business process. This kind of fun can lead to good results when it has a purpose and a goal. Team members laugh as they see how convoluted some of the process paths can become and discover how some of their business scenarios might go dreadfully wrong. Nervous laughter is often heard as they prepare their first performance for the executive audience. In the approval performances, it's common to hear the audience roaring with laughter when they see the "order from hell" being performed. That's the scenario that never happens in their organization!

Word gets out to the rest of the organization: "This business process design stuff is kind of neat; people are having fun doing it." People become interested in the design project, and it becomes the kind of project in which they'd like to participate. When people are chosen to be on these projects, they know that they will be able to see and understand more about the organization. They are at the cutting edge of progress and change in your organization and they can have fun. These feelings can be invaluable to the change management challenges that lie ahead.

Process Visualization produces an environment where people engage in serious play. Fun and laughter are a natural part of performing the processes. They are contagious and they produce results!

Create the Focus of a Clearly Defined Objective

Nothing focuses the team's attention more than knowing that they will be performing their proposed process design in front of an executive audience. Giving people a deadline to finish their design or a stack of documentation that needs to be developed is not as effective as giving them the objective of performing their proposed new business process design to their executive. Process Visualization has taught them to perform the processes for themselves, because that's how they developed the design. So it isn't as if the performance for the key stakeholders and executives will be a new and unknown act. This performance is conducted to gain the approval necessary to take the design into the implementation phase. The goal of completing the design project with a final performance is very effective at galvanizing the team's attention throughout the project. It's no longer good enough to just hand in a stack of documentation that few can be bothered to read and understand. Now, the objective is to bring the most senior level in the organization up to a level of understanding where they can confidently approve the next step—the risky part of the change initiative. Process Visualization gives the design team a tangible objective, one that they can clearly focus on as they start the design project.

Gain the Insight to Evaluate New Ideas and Technologies

Have you ever heard this kind of conversation within your organization: "Do our sales reps need to be supported by wireless technology in front of our customers? How will it help our customers? How can it support the sales process? Can wireless really support our sales effort when our sales rep is in front of the customer, or are we considering it simply to impress customers with our ability to track their order status while they sit across from us? But customers could do this themselves on the Internet. But maybe this wireless connection could really help our service people as their day changes due to the timing of the calls. But why can't they just talk to the dispatcher?" While this line of questioning is valid, do you ever feel that you are running in circles to find the answers?

Wouldn't the following comments be much more productive? "Our sales reps are involved in 10 major processes when they are in front of our customers. I can visualize four areas where wireless technologies might give them better support and timely information that could shorten the timeline of the sales process and close the deal faster. Maybe we should simulate a few scenarios and see what it looks like."

Process Visualization can give you the insight to evaluate where new technologies can best support your business. When you understand your business processes, you can better relate how new technologies could be used to support them. Technology is the vehicle that enables organizations to more effectively conduct their business and make them more competitive. When a new technology that merits a closer look emerges, the first thing to discover is where and how it could be used to better support or change your business processes. The more you understand your processes, the easier it is to spot the opportunities to use new technologies. The necessary support from the executive to further explore the opportunities is reached in a less painful and more knowledgeable way when everyone is able to see where in the business process the improvements and benefits can be realized.

The insight gained from knowing your current processes can also help you understand how new concepts and new business models will require a whole new set of processes. Process Visualization gives you the ability to better evaluate new ideas by relating them to how and where they will support business processes. It is this simple focus on the foundations of your business that can give you the ability to think at a strategic level and decide where the opportunities lie to make new concepts work for you.

CHAPTER THREE

Why Strive Towards Process Culture?

What does "Process Culture" mean? Becoming a Process Culture entails an organization reaching a stage where processes are naturally embedded in its management style. There are different stages that organizations progress through to become a Process Culture. Process Visualization can help your organization progress along the path to becoming a fully functioning Process Culture.

What Does a Process Culture Look Like?

An organization is said to be a Process Culture when business processes are naturally embedded in its thinking, lexicon, and decision-making. From creating new ideas to the ongoing work of improving current practices, processes are a natural part of thinking about how to make things work better. The efficiency and effectiveness of an organization is achieved as a result of ensuring that the business processes, people, and technology work together to achieve a common vision. New technologies are introduced only once there is an understanding of their impact on the people and processes that they will support.

People are organized into major process groups that are headed by a process owner. Compensation is linked to achieving process goals. The process owners ensure that the current processes support the business while they explore continuous improvements and experiment with new business models and enabling technologies. Whether the process owners are involved in designing and implementing a project that only affects their process scope or are working together on a program with a broader scope, they always ensure that everyone on the team understands how the changes fit into the business process structure that defines the organization's vision.

Organizations with a strong Process Culture employ a common process methodology. Consistency in discussing the elements and structure of business processes is facilitated by a common language. This doesn't make their approach to new concepts rigid. Rather, it makes their discussions and designs more flexible by incorporating ways of thinking about processes and ways of better expressing the possibilities of how they could operate. The people in a Process Culture employ their process methodology to become knowledgeable about current processes and thus prepared to tackle change initiatives involving new concepts and technologies. Their training has emphasized an understanding of the broader process relationships as well as the specifics of particular processes. They are specialists in some process areas and generalists in others. They are ready to participate as team members on process design projects.

Process Cultures are able to rapidly respond to changes in business conditions. Their people are ready for change because they are trained and familiar with using a common process language. In fact, they thrive on it. Process Cultures play, experiment, and have fun with new ideas. Their common language gives them the freedom and speed to communicate how new concepts will affect their organization and impact their customers. Process Cultures are often the technology innovators described in business journals and books.

An organization becomes a Process Culture when the executive leads the way. Process Culture does not just happen. The challenge to establish a process-centric environment within the whole organization requires a consistent and determined approach. Leadership, change management, organizational development, and training are all required to achieve this goal. Process Visualization has a small but important role to play in assisting an organization to become a Process Culture.

A handful of companies are most often mentioned whenever process innovation is discussed. These include 3M, American Express, Barclay Bank, Boeing, Dell, General Electric, IBM, Merck, Motorola, Proctor & Gamble, Sony, Texas Instruments, and Wal-Mart. Some of these organizations would admit that they are only successful in some divisions; all would say they are still learning and working to perfect their ideal of Process Culture. You don't have to be a large multi-national organization to become a Process Culture and enjoy the benefits. It isn't their size or their industry that causes these organizations to be written and talked about. It's their attitude towards their people and processes—and how they treat their people and organize both people and processes to achieve alignment with their business objectives.

The Maturity Stages of a Process Culture

Do you consider your organization to be a Process Culture? You can examine your organization and quickly determine where you are in the progression to becoming a Process Culture. Diagram 3.1 explains the different stages at which an organization may find itself along the path to becoming a Process Culture. Where would you place your organization today?

50

Diagram 3.1   The Maturity Stages
of a Process Culture

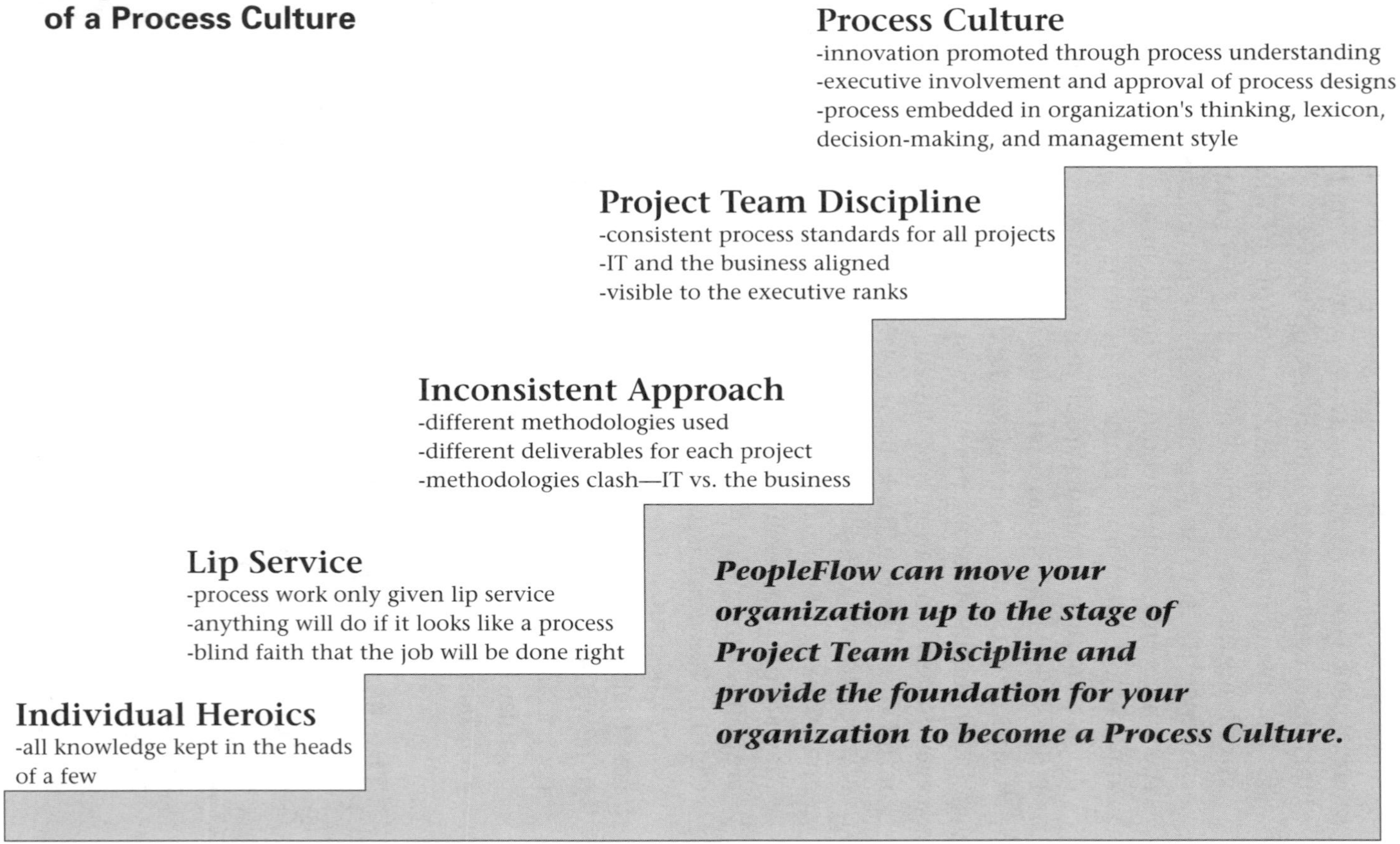

Process Culture
-innovation promoted through process understanding
-executive involvement and approval of process designs
-process embedded in organization's thinking, lexicon, decision-making, and management style

Project Team Discipline
-consistent process standards for all projects
-IT and the business aligned
-visible to the executive ranks

Inconsistent Approach
-different methodologies used
-different deliverables for each project
-methodologies clash—IT vs. the business

PeopleFlow can move your organization up to the stage of Project Team Discipline and provide the foundation for your organization to become a Process Culture.

Lip Service
-process work only given lip service
-anything will do if it looks like a process
-blind faith that the job will be done right

Individual Heroics
-all knowledge kept in the heads of a few

An Organization of Individual Heroes

At this first stage, most of an organization's process knowledge is kept in the heads of a few individuals, often long-service employees. They naturally became the oracles on how things work. They are consulted frequently when things go wrong. Knowledge becomes status because few things are ever documented. New people are trained by sitting and watching how systems work and how work activity flows. Often departing employees are the ones doing the training.

The executives don't understand the significance of the words "process" or "standard operating procedures." To them, it seems obvious that work activities should just naturally happen. If they've invested in new computer technology, then they expect it to solve all their problems. The implementation of new technology is done by the "systems people," who install the software and train the users on its features and functionality. Continuous improvement projects are hard to find, but there is a lot of talk about the need to cut costs. Projects that examine processes in an effort to understand and enhance them rarely happen. Any improvements to the operations are done in silos and usually on an opportunistic basis. Integration is never really considered, nor is the impact that changes have on people or processes.

Lip Service

At this stage, attempts at process design work are given lip service by people at all levels in the organization. But the feeling still persists that processes occur naturally, so there's no need to spend a great deal of time on them, especially when a large systems implementation project is looming. Everyone rushes to get into the systems and technology work with the belief that because best practices are in a new system's functionality, all that needs to be done is to incorporate them into the end-user training. Everyone talks as though processes are being considered in the implementation because this popular word is bantered about. Nothing concrete, however, is ever done with the business processes.

Any documentation that exists to explain proposed new processes involved in the systems project resembles simple concept diagrams. Current processes may be documented with Standard Operating Procedures (SOPs) that focus on specific job tasks in some areas. It's assumed that an integrated picture of business processes can be obtained by reading all the SOPs.

The executive's attitude is not very different from the previous stage of maturity. They still believe that things will work out well when new technologies are implemented. The concepts sound good, and since many other companies have implemented these systems before, why won't it work here, they reason? The organization is not an early adopter of new technologies, and so takes reassurance in knowing that they are not breaking new ground with the technology implementation.

Once they are in the middle of a systems implementation project, however, executives often begin to hear from the implementation team and end-users that their organization is unique. They hear comments like, "We don't work like that here." A disparity appears between what the executives believed and what they are now being told. The executives thought that they could simply install a new system and use its best practices. Members on the implementation team are not so sure of that approach because they have realized that the best practices in the system will cause changes that will fundamentally alter the way the organization conducts business. Also, the team sees that there are a number of ways that the best practices can be configured in the software. The implementation team lacks the authority to make these kinds of decisions and changes. The executive now begins to wonder if their organization is unique and if the system really does need to be modified. Trying to decide which is the best way to go is frustrating. The problem is this: There isn't a broader perspective from which to view how the business should best operate.

If you have determined that your organization is at the Lip Service stage, then you may have experienced some degree of turmoil during systems implementations. Perhaps you had the feeling that there might have been a better way to proceed before you became entangled in a large technology implementation.

The Inconsistent Approach

You want to become an organization that designs processes first and then goes on to implement the technology enablers. Your organization wants to keep pace with technology and maintain a competitive advantage in your marketplace. There's a lot happening right now throughout the organization; it's an exciting place to be. Many projects are underway, but it's beginning to seem to you that each one is being conducted differently. Whenever a project team shows you what they are proposing to do, it looks different from the previous presentation. Does every team have to look at their processes so differently? What if it doesn't all work together? Nobody appears to have the responsibility of ensuring that the End-to-End business processes are integrated. It's up to you to figure out how to understand all those different ways of documenting process designs if you want that integrated view of your business processes. The IT group is complaining because everyone is doing things so differently that it makes their task of interpreting the process designs difficult.

The executive is trying to show an interest in process concepts. Each executive member wants to give more attention to process and has encouraged his or her people to go out and learn more. Some projects have brought in consulting groups for their experience in the technology and systems, but each consulting group brings in a different approach to business process design. Inconsistency and lack of a common language is blocking the organization's ability to discuss, design, and implement integrated processes and technologies. Everything still appears to be done in silos. In the end, although everyone is sincere about getting more into process design, even the executives are unsure about what it is they are being asked to look at and approve. Technology implementation proceeds, but with a sense of trepidation on the part of some executives.

If your organization is at the Inconsistent Approach stage, it's time to standardize and be consistent throughout the organization.

Project Team Discipline

You have adopted a standardized and consistent process design methodology for your organization. Your business and IT people agree on the techniques and how the processes will be documented before they are passed on for technical design work and systems implementation. Everyone on the process design project is trained and certified on the process methodology and documentation standards. Your teams talk the same language. Process documentation lives on past the design project. It's used by the technology team to help select systems and software packages that best fit your process designs. They also use it in their pilots and testing before the system goes live. The business processes are used to develop and provide training to the users. It's incorporated into the training materials for new employees. All current documentation showing your As-Is processes is accessible and available to employees. All process standards are available to any employee to help them learn, understand, and follow process flows.

Continuous improvement projects that bring about incremental changes, as well as process and technology innovations that cause step changes, use the same process design techniques. They both trigger the As-Is process documentation to be consistently updated so that it's always current and available.

The executive is gaining confidence about approving business processes. Processes are presented to them in a consistent way. The design walk-through of a newly proposed process is still demanding, but how the processes are depicted is no longer a mystery. Executives who want a more detailed review of the design can be guided from a high level down to any level of detail that they desire to understand. Having the design team perform the business processes makes it easier for the executives to gain a clear understanding of how things are going to operate when the new system is implemented.

Project Team Discipline is an important stage on the way to developing a Process Culture. If you rank yourself here, then you are now ready to take the final step.

Process Culture

The final step up to becoming a Process Culture occurs when everyone recognizes that the executives of an organization are consistently promoting innovation and change in their business practices through process understanding. When executives passionately embrace process thinking, they are able to promote innovation more confidently when implementing new technologies. Even without a technical knowledge of new systems, executives will have an increased confidence in the ability of new systems to deliver results, since they will have an understanding of where and how the technology supports the business process. Process thinking becomes embedded in the activities of everyone involved in the process design projects. At this stage, it's easier for the design team to explain their proposals for process change, and it's easier for the executive to understand and approve them.

Support and staffing for both innovative process design projects and continuous improvement projects come from the process owners. The process owners take responsibility for their process changes. They also take responsibility to ensure that their processes stay integrated with those of other process owners. The management and the people within the organization have been re-aligned to a process-oriented structure.

The CIO and the Information Technology (IT) group can better explain to their peers why they wish to explore new technologies. By relating the new technologies to how they will improve business processes, the IT group gains early support as they explore and investigate new technology products. With the business process documentation readily available, it is easy to show exactly where the impact to process activities is expected.

Every business change initiative starts with a process design project that is well represented by analysts from the IT group. The CIO does not approve software purchases or systems development without the executives understanding and approving how the business processes will be impacted and improved. For their part, the process owners would not contemplate running a process design project without representation from the IT group that is certified in the process design methodology. The traditional friction between business and IT is less prevalent than in other organizations because the design of business processes and technology enablers is conducted as a partnership.

Process Culture, E-culture, and Emerging Technologies

The Internet has captured people's imaginations and conjured up a myriad of application possibilities. Media reports and marketing campaigns are full of success stories about organizations that are technology innovators. There is much discussion about ways in which the power of the Internet will change the way we do business. New hyphenated words have appeared at a rapid rate; first all the "e" words came into our vocabulary and now "m-commerce" and "c-commerce" are here. Many are proposing new business models and innovative companies are experimenting and piloting these concepts. Most business people agree that electronic business will be of benefit and that the new technologies will continue to advance, become more commonplace, and challenge us to adopt them.

Technology Gets All the Attention!

Unfortunately, emerging technologies steal the spotlight and media attention and business processes are, for the most part, lost in the rush to implement the latest systems. Technology has the sizzle, and in comparison, business processes seem dull and boring. Everyone crowds around to see the latest wireless device or the software's new functionality. But bring out a process chart to walk through, and eyes start to glaze over. Processes can be made more interesting and draw the attention that they deserve and require—before the technology is brought in to enable them. Process Visualization attempts to change this balance by making business processes more interesting to people. In a Process Culture, that balance has already been achieved between the key elements of people, process, and technology.

Lessons from the Recent Past

If we forget about people and process and only concentrate on technology, then we are forgetting about our recent history. Do you remember when Enterprise Resource Planning (ERP) systems first started to make their appearance in the mid-80s and by the early 90s were on every business's list of must-haves? Organizations were in such a rush to implement that they spent millions of dollars before stumbling and realizing that things were not going well. They were moving so fast that they either forgot about or rushed through business process design. They thought that the functionality in the ERP systems contained the latest best practices and simply had to be implemented. This mistake was a costly one. Some organizations are still trying to get it right today and have not yet achieved integration of their ERP systems and business processes. The failure of ERP implementations became news and were a major catalyst that helped emphasize the importance of business processes and the high cost of ignoring them.

Our mistakes show us that successfully enabling business processes does not just happen by implementing technology. Our focus needs to remain on the integration of all technology components with the business processes. People, process, and technology all need to be considered in a balanced approach. Business processes have as important a place in e-technology implementations as they do in ERP implementations.

Process Culture and E-Culture

Process Culture and e-culture are not at odds with each other. The recognition that Process Culture plays a key role in e-culture is not a totally foreign notion. Authors of e-culture books are dedicating sections and complete chapters to the role of business processes. Few go into the details of how to design and test the links between technology and process, but the topic is receiving attention. The promise of the new technologies is that they can redefine, transform, or eliminate the assumptions, inefficiencies, and redundancies that are embedded within current business processes. Process Culture and e-culture complement each other.

Becoming a Process Culture

You can make the quantum leap to the stage of Project Team Discipline. At which stage on the maturity scale did you place your organization? If you are at one of the first three stages, please don't get the impression that you have to pass through every one of the other stages in order to arrive at the Project Team Discipline stage. But you do have to reach the level of Project Team Discipline before you can become a Process Culture. Process Visualization can help you progress from any of the earlier stages to achieving Project Team Discipline. Process

Visualization can give your organization the boost that's needed for a quantum leap to the staging point for your step up to becoming a Process Culture.

The Project Team Discipline step essentially gets your organization to the level of starting to "craft" business processes. Before any handcrafted object can be produced, specific tools and techniques must be mastered. Tips and lessons learned from experienced practitioners of the craft will take you quickly up the learning curve. The same is true with business processes. When performing business processes begins to take hold in your organization, you should start to hear the phrase "Let's go PeopleFlow it!" When your people start to use Process Visualization naturally, you have arrived at Project Team Discipline. It doesn't take long for project teams to achieve this stage. You can start to realize the benefits from intrinsically using PeopleFlow in a matter of months.

Executive Commitment

Achieving the full definition of a Process Culture is a result of achieving commitment from the executive to become a process-aligned organization. Cultural change usually moves from the top down through an organization. The style that the executive displays by their words and actions filters down to the people in an organization. It's important to realize that it is this executive style and not methodology that is the key to developing a successful Process Culture. No methodology on its own will ever change the culture of the organization. So, how do you get to the stage where your organization has embraced business process to the point where it is naturally embedded in its thinking, lexicon, decision-making, and management style?

Achieving a Process Culture is a result of achieving commitment from the executive to organize and operate in a process-aligned manner. There is no question that it takes involvement from a number of executive members to move the organization to the Project Team Discipline stage. A further commitment is now needed by the entire executive group to take the organization to the final step. It takes time to achieve a comfort level working in a Process Culture. It's not a skill that every executive naturally possesses or should be expected to possess. Since a Process Culture relies on you to promote innovation through process, you need to acquire the skills that will help you do that.

Process-Centred Executives

Executives need to be confident with process-centric thinking before altering the organization's management structure and style. Before you start to align your organization with your processes, or appoint process owners or tie compensation to process performance, you need to ensure that your organization is ready for this cultural shift. The entire executive should be confident that they are ready to take their organization in this direction. It will take a piloting approach and professional change management to fully accomplish this goal throughout your organization. You should seek guidance from organizational professionals as you consider how best to undertake this significant change in your organization's structure. An important key to getting started is establishing confidence in your abilities as a process-centric thinker and manager. These are the characteristics that will become evident to your staff members. This is the style they need to see in action in order to gain confidence in your direction. It's not good enough to just say you believe in a process-centric approach—you need to live it.

When your organization has reached the Project Team Discipline stage, the executive should be using Process Visualization concepts on all process change projects, no matter how small. Over time, and with a few projects completed, the executive will discover what works in their organization and what needs to be changed to fit the culture. Your own comfort level with directing and managing process-driven projects will increase if you participate in the informal as well as the formal process performance sessions. Spend some time reviewing the team's documentation and gain confidence by learning the simple principles behind Process Visualization. Once the confidence in process-centric thinking and management is evident in the executive group, you are ready to plan and pilot the alignment of the organization into process groups.

Why Do You Need to Get There?

Process Visualization is a small part of becoming a Process Culture. Its role is to get you thinking about and understanding how people, processes, and technology all work together to support business strategies and change initiatives. By forcing you to visualize the contact points and hand-offs that constantly occur between internal and external stakeholders, it indicates the places where you can leverage opportunities to gain further competitive advantage. I already discussed the benefits of using Process Visualization in your organization in Chapter 2. Even if you never become a completely process-aligned organization, there are many good reasons to use Process Visualization as your organization continues to change.

But why should you strive to take that last but important step that defines a Process Culture? Why align your people and organization around processes? Why become a process-managed and process-aligned organization? The answer to this question goes beyond the scope of this book. But it's a question that you will need to answer if you are to pursue Process Culture to its ultimate stage: a process-aligned organization. Further reading on this topic can be found in the Reference books and articles indicated by [3]. Here's a look at some of the reasons presented by other writers that you might consider.

- **Organizing around processes allows focused delivery of your value proposition.** When an organization is aligned around processes, it's able to more effectively direct its people, processes, and technologies towards the focused goal of producing and delivering its value proposition. The value proposition can be oriented towards products, or services, or both. By aligning to the value proposition, an organization becomes a more effective, robust, versatile, and finely-tuned delivery vehicle. Tailoring to produce and deliver individual value propositions to customers becomes more feasible, effective, and competitive.

- **A process-aligned organization is more flexible, adaptive, and responsive. It handles change better.** When an organization becomes aligned and managed along process lines, it is better able to handle change and, in fact, embraces it. These companies maintain their current processes, which successfully satisfy customers' demands, and, at the same time, they experiment with new ideas, technologies, and improvements that distinguish them from their competition.

- **The concept of a process-managed organization revolves around change.** Process-managed organizations allow their different business units to do things their own way and look carefully at the processes that work and those that do not. Piloting process changes and then sharing the ideas and their results through process councils is key to knowledge management and learning throughout the organization. Process-centric global organizations have effective ways of sharing ideas; they are able to cross the boundaries of language, culture, and functional expertise.

- **Changing from a traditional alignment reduces the persistent issues that face most function-aligned organizations.** You no doubt have heard of these problems and concerns before: protection of small fiefdoms, unproductive turf wars, overspecialization resulting in narrow thinking, and fragmentation of tasks lead to fragmentation of responsibilities. These common issues are often found in traditional function-aligned organizations.

These same issues tend to diminish when an organization becomes process-aligned. Process alignment in an organization may cause some of its own problems, but the persistent issues that afflict an otherwise productive and effective working environment will tend to diminish.

Starting on the Path to Becoming a Process Culture

Taking your organization all the way to a process-aligned management structure requires a major commitment. It's difficult for the organization to accept a process approach if the individuals in the organization have not yet experienced it. But achieving the maturity stage of Project Team Discipline is a low-risk, high-reward undertaking. If you are interested in starting on this path, then read on. I'll tell you more about PeopleFlow in the next chapter. The concepts of Process Visualization have been packaged in the PeopleFlow toolkit so that your organization can start to learn and use the concepts and quickly realize the benefits.

CHAPTER FOUR

What Is
PeopleFlow?

PeopleFlow is the toolkit that can give you a quick start to using the concepts of Process Visualization. As a toolkit, it provides a systematic approach for tackling the design and documentation of business processes. PeopleFlow makes it simple to grasp and evaluate business process designs and emerging technology concepts. It provides a solid foundation for process innovation and avoids leaving the design in an intellectualized state where only a few understand it. This approach allows stakeholders and executives to actively participate in the approval of their business process designs before committing significant resources to technology implementation projects.

PeopleFlow Makes a Business Process Come Alive

The central concept of Process Visualization and PeopleFlow is that business processes need to be brought to life. When you are able to experience the process, your interest level is raised and you understand and remember more about it. This is accomplished by transforming the business process into a Participative Theatre activity—one that can be watched and where interaction occurs. Think of the way that medical procedures have been revolutionized because of the ability of doctors to use MRI or ultrasound technologies to see inside the body. There is now a miniature camera that patients swallow to enable images of their digestive systems to be viewed. In the same way, a play based on your business processes has the ability to take you inside and show you the activities that accomplish the goal of a business process. Members of the design team are the actors: they perform the flow of the business process. People play a number of roles, including the parts of automated functions inside the software, manual tasks, physical operations, and the actions of stakeholders such as customers, suppliers, and decision-makers. Stage props are used to support the actors. Foam boards with sticky notes and labels represent information repositories, either computer databases or paper files. Smaller boards with key information posted on them are moved between the actors to show the information that each process requires as input and what it is expected to produce as output. For a supply chain process, stage props such as boxes of product, bar-coded labels, a laser pen acting as a scanner, a wagon substituting for an 18-wheeler tractor-trailer rig, and hats with corporate logos of customers, suppliers and service providers, all help to make PeopleFlow a compelling event. But don't think this is all just superficial role-playing; beneath the façade is a calculated seriousness. This serious play is work.

PeopleFlow sounds simple, and when it's done correctly, it is simple. You will come away with a much clearer understanding of your business processes. As a business process is performed, it literally unfolds before your eyes. The actors perform the activities that the process performs. They describe what they are doing as if they were that process activity going through its motions. You hear what actions need to occur, and sometimes why they need to happen this way. You literally see information flowing throughout the process to support all its activities. The actors add information on sticky notes to their board as they describe the information flow and its urgency in time. The need for key data elements to quickly support the business process becomes obvious. The importance of the timing and availability of the data emerges, as does an understanding of the technologies required to gather and deliver the information. It becomes apparent as you experience the performance that specific information requirements are what generate the technology requirements. By using PeopleFlow, information needs are understood by everyone who watches the flow of the process.

As an executive listening to and watching the business process flow, you might have some disturbing thoughts. You realize that there are parts of the business process that you want to question. You're concerned about some of the steps of a process and want to direct the team to rethink parts of it. You see that the direction given to the team or the policies and business rules being showcased need to be refined at an executive level before they are given back to the team. The questioning and subsequent refinements are all positive for both the business processes and the design team.

Everyone involved in major business change initiatives wants the design to be right. Reworking the business process designs is an expected part of the design cycle. It's common to go back to the design step after the executives have seen the proposed new business processes. When you thoroughly understand something, it's natural to realize that some of your initial thoughts were a bit off base and others need to be refined. It's a compliment to the team that senior executives and key stakeholders actually understand all their hard work and preparation. PeopleFlow has essentially made each participant an active member of the design process. After seeing the final PeopleFlow session, your thoughts will probably be similar to those of other observers: "My business process team really knows their stuff!" "More people in our organization need to experience this." Perhaps at the end of the session you'll leave with the thought, "I think we have a better chance of actually making this work; let's get into the implementation."

PeopleFlow Guides You Through the Business Process Design Project

When an organization undertakes a major business change initiative, it invariably involves implementing systems and technologies to support those changes. A major change means an organization wants to change its strategy, business model, or business practices. In most cases, the path to achieving the business change initiative involves a significant investment in technology, followed by a technology implementation program. Technology itself can be the reason to undertake change. More organizations want to explore the benefits of e-business initiatives as this technology becomes commonplace. In either case, the technology implementation program is never the end objective of the change initiative. It often receives most of the attention because it is often the riskiest, most expensive, and time-consuming part of the business change initiative. Technology implementation is always on the critical path. If it falters, drags on, or outright fails, then the business change initiative is doomed.

PeopleFlow recommends launching the business change initiative by conducting an initial project called the Business Process Design Project. Recall the analogy to the project conducted by products companies to design, prototype, simulate, test, and approve a new product before it is produced and launched. The Business Process Design Project should be viewed in the same light. This project should front-end your technology implementation program.

The deliverable of the Business Process Design Project is an executive-approved business process design that is ready to proceed to the next step and be enabled with technology and people. The design is a clear statement of how business processes need to operate and how systems are intended to support them in order for the business to meet the objectives of the change initiative and realize the benefits. The design provides everyone with a definitive statement of what the business needs to succeed. It is developed with team members from various areas of the business and members from the IT group to ensure that a feasible process design is achieved. It's not cast in stone, but it's intended to give everyone a clear roadmap of how to take the next step and proceed with the technology implementation.

A PeopleFlow-Driven Project Provides a Clear Objective for the Design Team

PeopleFlow gives the process design team an objective much like that of the creative team for theatre or a film—the opening night performance. A successful producer wants to create, produce, and stage a story that the audience will enjoy. A playwright wants the audience to learn something from the production. The director wants you to feel the experience and appreciate the professionalism of the cast. The actors themselves want to convey their characters to you in a memorable way. Everyone involved wants you to take away an experience that will lead to different ways of thinking and behaving. Now look at a Business Process Design Project in a similar light. In such a project, the team needs to create/design and write/document scripts that essentially tell the stories/processes of how business scenarios will play themselves out in the real world once they are implemented by the new processes and technologies.

Nothing focuses the team's attention more than knowing that they will be performing their proposed process design in front of an executive audience. The team knows that they must deliver a performance of their business process designs to executives, the Steering Committee, and other key stakeholders in the organization that are impacted by the project. Much depends on this performance: to gain approval to move the project on to the next phase. The team knows their audience will be alert and watching closely to gain a full understanding of their proposal for how the newly designed processes will work. They realize that they need to competently act out their parts so that their audience will appreciate the subtleties and creativity of their design. It's this goal that provides them with the clear objective and the culminating focus for all of their design work—from day one of the Business Process Design Project.

At this stage, it isn't as if the performing of processes is new and unknown to the team. Process Visualization has already taught them to perform the processes for themselves, as they developed the design throughout the project. Although they now need to perform in front of the key stakeholders and executives, all it takes is some refinement to make the performance smoother than their design sessions.

Team members soon realize that this approach is not like other design projects. It used to be that a team worked away for months and produced a pile of design documents that few people beyond the design team could comprehend. Often, little, if any, of the design ever saw the light of day, or got to implementation, because the key stakeholders did not understand, nor support it. The team also realizes that unlike a play performed in a theatre, the audience can question the actors and the script and suggest changes. The audience can send the performers back for rework and even demand another performance. Process Visualization is true interactive theatre!

The objective of the performances is to bring the executive up to a level of understanding where they can confidently approve the next step—the risky part of the change initiative. The prospect of this performance being held in front of the executives helps to galvanize the team. It's not good enough to just hand in that stack of documentation at the end of the project that few will bother to read. Process Visualization gives the team a valuable objective to achieve—one that the team can clearly focus on from the start.

PeopleFlow Provides a Framework for Documenting Business Processes

Supporting the performance style of PeopleFlow is a solid foundation of techniques. It's essential that the design team use these techniques as they develop the documentation for an integrated business process. As an executive, you won't need to get into the details of documenting business processes, but it's an essential part of the team's work. Setting and using simple standards is the key to keeping the design integrated. By using a common vocabulary, team members are encouraged to express and document new and innovative concepts in terms everyone can quickly grasp. In the creation or review of the documentation, common standards make it easier for everyone to quickly understand the essence of the design.

Process documentation and charting is not new. Various charting standards are readily available in software drawing packages, and PeopleFlow makes use of them. The standard shapes are familiar and have accepted meanings. The use of "swim lanes" to depict responsibility for tasks and to differentiate between manual and system-enabled tasks is also common and is employed in PeopleFlow's charting style. So how is the PeopleFlow documentation approach different? PeopleFlow distinguishes itself in two ways. First, it makes good use of various levels of charts. The levels are used to "peel the onion" and guide you from the big picture down through the layers of detail of the process design. The levels are well defined, and each one has a specific purpose during the design project. If you were to make a video to instruct people how to climb to the summit of a mountain, you would not start with a close-up of the trail. Rather, your first scene would show the entire mountain, and then you would begin to zoom in to familiarize the viewer with various aspects of the mountain's environment. What does the face of the mountain that the route will follow look like? Where are the glaciers and ridges? Finally, you would show the particulars of the route and emphasize the difficult sections that will be encountered. In the same way, PeopleFlow's structured style moves from the big picture to the details of a process design.

Secondly, PeopleFlow's style is unique in that its documentation and charts are structured using concepts that tell a story. PeopleFlow created concepts for its charts to help capture and convey process design more easily. They include the Mainline Path, Exception and Resolution Paths, Triggers, and Escalations. PeopleFlow charts are much more interesting and informative than the usual standard ones because the eye is skilfully guided through the flow of the process.

What PeopleFlow Is and What It Is Not

PeopleFlow is:	PeopleFlow is not:
• an essential *front-end* to a major business change initiative, involving technology implementation (selection/purchase/design/build/test/rollouts).	• a methodology to conduct the follow-on systems design and implementation project.
• focused on business processes, including their design and approval. It takes into account, at a high level, the technology that could be considered to enable the processes.	• focused on the details of the technologies and systems that can enable the business processes.
• an approach to effectively gain the understanding and approval of business processes and their policies and business rules by senior executives and stakeholders.	• an approach to a system walk-through, or a conference room pilot, or acceptance testing or sign-off/approval.

PeopleFlow is:	PeopleFlow is not:
• a way to ensure integrity and integration of End-to-End business processes.	• a systems integration methodology.
• a toolkit of simple and effective techniques to design new business processes as well as understand current processes.	• a replacement for any information system design methodology.
• a variety of techniques and templates to document a business process and make it easier to visualize and understand the complexities of the process.	• a replacement for any information system documentation methodology.
• a pragmatic approach to designing business processes that openly discusses all the iterations, rework, issues, and problems that inevitably happen during these projects.	• a theoretical approach, outlining how an ideal design and implementation project should happen.

You can see that PeopleFlow is meant to complement and "front-end" a major systems and technology design and implementation project. It does not replace IT methodologies, techniques, and documentation. It has the ability to enhance the understanding and relationships between the business users and technical systems designers. The Business Process Design Project can actually speed up the implementation. It allows the technical team to confidently move forward with their work, without the need to constantly have to recycle back to the business team.

Business processes and the systems that enable them go hand in hand. In PeopleFlow the team members in the Business Process Design Project include both business and systems representatives. Current processes are documented and new business processes are designed so that the technology enablers will be a well-represented part of the documentation. PeopleFlow recognizes that after the business process designs are completed, the systems team needs to quickly get into the technical aspects of the system design, acquisition, construction, and testing in order to fully enable the business processes. When the system implementation starts, the methodology, documentation techniques, and tools that are within your IT organization will start to gear up. The key advantage to a PeopleFlow-driven Business Process Design Project is that at this point the IT team fully understands the design. They have a process design approved by the business executives and a complete set of documentation to take forward into the rest of the implementation.

PeopleFlow Compared to a Traditional Design Approach

How does PeopleFlow compare to the traditional approach that is used to design business processes? The PeopleFlow approach is always to guide an organization through a Business Process Design Project. In the past, the concept of conducting a full process design project was often skipped by organizations eager to jump into the technology implementation. Nevertheless, most organizations spend some time in a design phase. Here is how PeopleFlow compares to the traditional approach of designing business processes:

PeopleFlow Approach:	Traditional Design Approach:
• **Open, participatory, and inclusive**	• **Often hidden, restricted, and inaccessible**
Stakeholders, executives, subject matter experts, and the design team are all active participants in refining the business process design. It can easily be opened up to customers and suppliers for their participation and review.	The design team is the only group familiar with the overall design. Few people in the organization understand the design. It is difficult for most executives to take the time to understand the design.
• **Extremely visual**	• **Not visual**
Performing the business processes lets everyone see and hear how the processes work. Key pieces of documentation are displayed and presented for everyone to see. Documentation is also kept in computers and binders.	Documentation is kept in computers and binders out of sight of the rest of the organization. Little attempt is made to display information.
• **Performing the business processes lets everyone experience the design.**	• **Walk-throughs with charts are the principal means to explain designs.**
Business processes are brought to life as they are performed. Everyone in the audience is better able to grasp the essence and details of the design. The audience can participate in discussions on design refinements and issues	The design team explains their work by walking others through the process charts and describing what happens. This makes it tough to hold the audience's attention long enough to really explain

PeopleFlow Approach:	Traditional Design Approach:
arising from the new business process design.	the design. People find the design difficult to grasp.
• **Integrated business process design is more readily assured.** Techniques in PeopleFlow focus on continually cross-checking the design as it develops to ensure that it is integrated end-to-end across processes, as well as vertically integrated down through the levels of detail in each process. Integration is a key focus for all team members.	• **Integration is not assured.** There is no formal mechanism to assure that all the processes and information flows are integrated before handing the design over to the technical implementation. The design often appears to have been done in silos by different groups on the design team.
• **The design team is trained and certified.** Training and certification ensures that all team members can participate fully and support each other from the start of the design project. Teams use the same common language for expressing their designs and the same documentation formats.	• **Usually no formal team training is conducted.** It is often assumed that team members seconded from their positions in the business can design processes because they have been involved with the process every day. They usually receive nothing more than instructions on how to use the software drawing package to draw the process charts.

PeopleFlow Approach:	Traditional Design Approach:
• An approved business process design by the executive signals the completion of the design project. The executive knows their role is to understand and approve the design before it moves into the next phase of implementation. The design team knows that they must gain approval through their final performance of the design to the executive. The project has clear milestones that everyone understands.	• The design project is finished when the team feels they have achieved a good process design. There is no clear event that signals the end of the design project. Usually the project ends when the team finally feels confident about their design, and they hand in a pile of documentation.

Frequently Asked Questions about PeopleFlow

Q: I thought my software vendor and systems integrator already had a solid implementation methodology to follow. They consider business processes in their methodology. Where does PeopleFlow fit in?

A: PeopleFlow is not a cookie-cutter approach aimed at the implementation of any particular software package or technology. At a certain stage of any system implementation it is essential to get into the details of the system. But, there is a step that needs to be done, and done right, and it should happen at the beginning of all implementation programs. It's the Business Process Design Project. Make sure that the methodology you are going to follow contains this step. Your first project in the program needs to be primarily focused on business process integration and secondarily on technology. It needs to have a thorough method to design, simulate and test, and approve your business processes. It needs to show you the big picture; ensure you that relationships with customers and suppliers are enhanced; and, finally, satisfy you that people, processes, and all the various technologies will be truly integrated. Make sure that the concepts of Process Visualization are incorporated so that executives can *actively* be involved in the approval process.

Q: How does PeopleFlow fit in with what our IT group uses to design and document systems? Does this get replaced or changed in any way if we use PeopleFlow?

A: PeopleFlow is not a replacement for any systems development methodology. To start a systems project, your IT analysts probably try to collect a list of user requirements before purchasing, developing, or modifying a system. Think of PeopleFlow documentation as the most complete list of user requirements that an IT analyst could ever dream of collecting. If your organization uses Joint Application Design (JAD) sessions to get users and IT both involved in a new system, think of PeopleFlow's performing of business processes as a super JAD session. If you use prototyping to develop new applications with your users, then PeopleFlow produces a highly developed initial prototype that can then be taken and developed further using the technology. PeopleFlow does not replace what your IT group uses today when they start the systems work of designing, developing, and documenting the technology part of a system.

What PeopleFlow does do is provide the entire organization with a front end for developing and documenting what the business needs from the technology and how it will be used once it's implemented.

Q: Isn't it better to use the new system, since it's already been purchased, to guide us through our business process designs? We don't want to be going off on tangents in the Business Process Design Project and doing things that the package can't handle!

A: If you have already committed to a packaged solution, it's still your best option not to use it solely as your guide to business process design. But this is a serious issue for the Steering Committee to answer, and it's dependent on the scope that they give the design team. By looking only at the package's capabilities, you are choosing to limit your options. Remember that the Business Process Design Project is the opportunity to explore what your business needs to be successful, not just what a single software package in its current version has to offer. It's better to examine what the business requires, not what the business has to learn to live with. Exploring your true business requirements and then comparing them to the package you have purchased is valuable. It's useful to have an application consultant, who is knowledgeable about the software package, as part of your project team. There may be new ideas in the package that can help your thinking and design. Alternately, there may be valuable concepts and features that you require that could be developed by the package vendor for the next release of the package. A partnership will form between you and your technology vendor. Don't be afraid to leverage this opportunity or to explore beyond the boundaries of the software package.

Q: PeopleFlow and Process Visualization seem so simple and intuitive. Why can't we just try it out ourselves right now? Is there a lot more about it to be learned? Do I really need to put my team through a training class?

A: The concepts are very simple. That is the key to their success. PeopleFlow was assembled as a toolkit to give your teams a quick start and prevent them from having to reinvent the wheel and learn as they go from their mistakes. There are techniques to learn about how to facilitate and conduct design sessions when using the Participative Theatre technique. There is much to learn about properly documenting business processes. Learning the foundation of Process Thinking is vital for the team to work together and succeed. The components of Process Thinking include the building blocks of processes, the common language, and elements that compose a business process.

Q: I'm not so sure that PeopleFlow would fit into our culture. Our people seem pretty conservative and probably would not want to perform in front of executives. Will it work for us?

A: People are always worried at first about performing in front of each other. That is why PeopleFlow uses icebreaker exercises that get people comfortable with performing. Once they get started, you would be amazed at how people catch on and transform into lively actors. Even quiet and reserved people like the PeopleFlow style, because it allows them a forum in which to have their say over their more assertive colleagues who often attempt to dominate traditional design sessions. With PeopleFlow, everyone gets to express his or her ideas.

Case History: How a Major North American Retailer Used PeopleFlow

A major North American retailer used PeopleFlow to guide their organization through a Business Process Design Project that was the front end to a large supply chain change initiative. The corporation is currently in the midst of their planned multi-year implementation program. They have requested that their organization not be identified while the new processes and technologies are being rolled out. The corporation is a leading hard goods retailer with sales approaching $5 billion. It offers consumers over 100,000 products through a network of over 400 stores. The corporate offices and retail stores employ nearly 40,000 people.

Growth Through Their Change Initiative Is a Key Corporate Strategy

Early in 1999 when the corporation was confident that its Y2K effort was well on the way to meeting its deadlines, work to further enhance its supply chain capabilities got underway. A major business change initiative was launched with the objective to provide business process and technology enhancements that would lead to multi-channel, regional distribution. The goal was to give the corporation a significant increase in supply chain capacity, higher inventory turns, reduced product handling, and lower transportation costs. Currently the corporation operates from warehouses in one centralized geographical area. Regional distribution will mean opening new facilities in other parts of North America in order to have product closer to the stores. But even that will not provide the supply chain capacity needed to support the growth. By moving to a multi-channel supply chain, the capacity requirements and the other supply chain goals can be achieved.

Currently, products move predominantly through the warehouses in what is referred to as the Storage channel, with a few products being shipped direct from suppliers to the stores. The objective of the multi-channel capability is to implement a four-channel design that will add the Cross Dock and Flow-through Channels and increase products in the Direct Ship Channel. In the new Cross Dock Channel, a supplier picks and packs their products to fulfill individual store orders and then ships them all together to a corporate warehouse. When this combined shipment of individual store orders arrives at the warehouse, it is not put into storage. The orders are sorted, moved directly from the receiving dock to the shipping dock, and put on the appropriate truck destined to each of the stores. This channel increases supply chain capacity by reducing the amount of handling required in the warehouse. The Flow-through Channel is intended to increase to capacity to move high-volume products effectively through the warehouse. When a full trailer load of a flow-through product arrives, it is not put into storage. Instead, store orders are picked directly from the trailer onto the receiving dock, moved directly from the receiving dock to the shipping dock, and put on the appropriate truck destined to each of the stores. These four channels are designed to move products from the suppliers to the stores in the most efficient manner for each type of product. Without effective processes and systems, the efficient movement of product in these four channels cannot be achieved. Designing and implementing the business processes and technologies that are required to support each of the channels is the challenge for the change initiative.

The Implementation Program Is Formed and Launched

Although the legacy systems successfully took the corporation over the Y2K hurdle, the goal was always to replace them with newer Enterprise Resource Planning (ERP) systems. The corporation formed a team to evaluate available ERP packages in the marketplace. The corporation already was a user of a well-known Advanced Planning System (APS) and is a key reference site for the APS vendor. The corporation was to implement the use of more modules and functionality in the APS to enable the processes that support operations planning and achieve a key goal in the change initiative. The real challenge, then, was to replace the transactional systems with newer software and hardware. The corporation selected and purchased an ERP system for its order processing, inventory, and purchasing software. The Supply Chain group had already spent quality time with the concepts of the four-channel design and had developed a high-level flow of the processes, but from the supply chain perspective only. It was recognized that the corporation had not yet conducted a Business Process Design Project that went into enough detail on all the processes and technologies that would be impacted by the implementation of the new design. It was time to back up a little and formulate a program to direct all the work that would be required to make the implementation a success. The implementation program was launched and staffed with commitment and support from the executive. A Program Director was selected, and she staffed a program office to ensure that planning and monitoring of this sizable program would be successful. A Steering Committee was formed with members at the highest executive level in the corporation. Because the program was so large, a Working Committee was formed with membership at the director level. The first project in the program was the Business Process Design Project.

The Business Process Design Project needed to tackle a broad scope in a short period of time. To accomplish this, the design teams were selected from all the areas impacted in the corporation. This resulted in a design team of 50 people, of which the majority were dedicated full time to the project. Seven process teams were formed to tackle the business processes directly involved in the scope of the program—Store Order Management, Purchase Order Management, Inventory, Warehouse Management, Transportation Management, Demand Forecasting and Replenishment, and Operations and Transportation Planning. Three Marketing teams and two Finance teams were formed to consider those processes impacted by the project: Promoting a Product, Cost and Price, Assortment Planning, Billing and A/R, and A/P. IT and the business both had good representation on the teams. An Integration Team was formed to ensure that the design would remain tightly integrated throughout the project. The scope of the program was considerable in magnitude, and the best people had been assigned to the design teams. A program kick-off introduced the goals of the change initiative to the organization. Then, the Business Process Design Project kick-off was held for the design team to become familiar with the challenges ahead. The change initiative was on its way!

PeopleFlow Guides the Business Process Design Project

The Business Process Design Project started without using PeopleFlow. It soon became apparent that in order to co-ordinate so many design teams with a scope encompassing a large part of the organization's core business processes and involving many stakeholders, including the dealers, that a simple but comprehensive methodology was needed. PeopleFlow was selected by the corporation to direct the Business Process Design Project. It was the largest project PeopleFlow had guided at that time.

The team members were given training on the PeopleFlow techniques; then the work got underway. Because of the extensive re-engineering work that had already taken place within the supply chain, a number of the As-Is business processes were already documented. However, the Marketing and Finance teams found that this project was a good opportunity to document their As-Is processes using the PeopleFlow style of documentation. Validating the As-Is was not a difficult task, and the teams eagerly moved into the To-Be design.

The To-Be design got underway with the Integration Facilitator leading the Process Team Leaders and a few senior team members through the design of the high-level processes that structure the design. These team leaders developed a Context Chart to give a clear perspective of all the processes involved in the change initiative. The team leaders also developed initial cuts of the End-to-End process flows to show the major scenarios that needed to be supported. Next, the work was chunked out and the work packages used to control the work were defined and approved.

It took team members some time to become familiar with performing their process flows instead of just discussing them. People were shy and tentative at first. To get the team loosened up and into the mood for performing business processes, we conducted the Licks Burger warm-up exercise. Licks is a burger chain that has an interesting process for taking your order and then moving it through their production-line process. It's always fun to see people discover all the subtle nuances and process details that make this simple, yet effective, process such an interesting one to view and then simulate. After this exercise, the team started to get more comfortable with performing, and soon the technique started to take hold. The teams were using performance in their design meetings and at the integration meetings to develop the designs. Designing business processes using PeopleFlow was starting to be an effective tool.

The To-Be design always takes awhile before you actually see it all coming together. The experience on this project was no different. The high-level charts and design concepts were all completed in a relatively short period of time. However, the work of getting further into the process details, the information flows, and the integration of all the component parts took many months to get right. But as the teams started to refine their documentation for each work package, and as the process performances became smoother and more complete, the details of the proposed design emerged for all to see and experience. When the entire team reached agreement that their design was complete, they were ready to unveil it. It was time to take the proposed process design to the stakeholders and Steering Committee for their review, suggested changes, and approval. The first round of the approval process had begun in the Business Process Design Project.

The team selected the End-to-End process flows for each of the four channels for their executive performances. They rehearsed diligently to fine-tune the processes to the point where the actors were smoothly discussing the processes, information flow, and rationale for their activities. The transitions between actors from one activity to the next were crisp; they didn't lose a beat during the performance. The team was nervous but ready for their performance date with the stakeholders and executives.

The audience consisted of 10 senior executives (stakeholders and Steering Committee members) and two store representatives. The performances were held over one-and-a-half days. Not a single member of the audience missed a minute of the entire performance. In the first performance the team managed to pull their audience right into the process content, and from then on things really started to happen. There was a lot of laughter over the day and a half of performances. The audience loved the honesty and humour when the team did their "Order from Hell" routine. In this scenario, everything that possibly could go wrong with the store order did. Of course, everyone in the audience joked that it could never happen here!

There were serious moments as well. The executive saw how much information had to flow between the stores and the corporation in order to process different types of orders. Everyone agreed that this issue would have to be investigated further, to see how to reduce this volume of data flow and yet retain the high level of information requirements. Still in the back of people's minds was the concern that the proposed process design and the functionality of the purchased software were not in sync in a number of areas. This would need to be resolved in the Conference Room Pilot (CRP). The team formulated different business process options to take into the CRP to help address this.

At the end of the performances the team was given a warm applause and congratulation from the entire audience. More importantly, the process design was approved to move into the next phase of the implementation program, which was the Conference Room Pilot. Obtaining approval concluded the Business Process Design Project and advanced the change initiative forward to its next phase.

PeopleFlow Continues to Be Used at This Corporation

"Let's PeopleFlow it!" is a phrase that continues to be used at this corporation. There are always a number of smaller design projects and continuous improvement efforts on the go. Because PeopleFlow proved to be such a success, it continues to be the method of choice to design business processes. And people conduct their PeopleFlow sessions on their own, without the need for further consulting support. Even within the change initiative, PeopleFlow was put to use again. This time the business processes were performed for the ERP software vendor so that their designers could better understand the need for modifications to their system's functionality. After performing the four-channel design, the software designers understood the need for change. Also, how the software needed to change was better defined for everyone involved. PeopleFlow made the gap analysis easier for the both the Information Technology team and for the software vendor's design team.

Lessons Learned

While it's interesting to read about how a Business Process Design Project was conducted and reached a successful conclusion, it's also important to learn from the successes and issues that occurred during the project.

The Project Got Off to a "Trickle Start," Which Made It More Difficult for Everyone Involved

Because there were 13 teams, a large number of people needed to be brought on to the project. Getting everyone on-board did not happen all at once because some people had previous commitments. The project ramped up slowly in numbers, which meant multiple training and orientation sessions. Although some parts of the design started before everyone was on-board, eventually all the teams achieved their full complement. Trickle starts to large projects are not unusual when so many people are needed all at once. Keep this situation in mind when you plan your projects.

At First the Teams Did Not Realize the Difference in Roles That Was Required of Them

Some teams were working on processes directly involved in the project's scope while others worked on processes that could be potentially impacted by the scope. The people on these two different types of process teams were required to participate differently in the design process. Team members eventually became comfortable taking on different styles of participating and designing. People found it easier to be working on a process directly involved in the project's scope. Marketing and Finance were the "impacted" processes. This meant that these teams did not redesign their processes unless it was absolutely necessary to integrate them with the newly designed in-scope processes. There was a natural tendency to attempt to improve and redesign all processes! Merely observing the design to see if some interesting idea or activity in a process is going to impact you is difficult. The impacted teams had to determine what new information would be available as input to their impacted processes and then assess if this would be helpful to them. Also, the in-scope teams asked them for more information to be sourced from their processes so that the in-scope processes could be improved. Often the impacted team would struggle to supply the requested information without making significant changes to their processes. Eventually, the two teams got these different dynamics down to an art, and the design of key information flows throughout the integrated design moved along smoothly.

Make sure that your team members are aware of the two different roles that are expected of them. It's not usually feasible to change everything in an organization in one change initiative. Some people need to take the less active role of observing how the new designs of the in-scope processes are unfolding and how they will affect their processes.

The Transactional Software Package Had Been Purchased Prior to the Design Project and Caused Some Debate About Fit

"Are we designing our future processes to match the software's capabilities or to accomplish our business requirements?" The software vendor had consultants on site to assist with the team's understanding of ERP software's feature/functionality. But some teams kept running into the perception that the software would not support the business processes that they were designing. What were they to do? Were the teams supposed to design and document their proposed business process in the manner they felt was required to achieve the business requirements, or were they to do their best to use the software's functionality and compromise on the business processes?

The issue needed clarification. The Program Director explained the direction to the team:

Our future design for business processes must meet business requirements and be flexible, fast, efficient, and cost-effective. The business requirements must be kept as the focus, while understanding how the systems can support the processes. If the teams choose to make any "accommodations" that affect business requirements, then the Steering Committee must approve this decision. In that case, the team must document the process that we would have designed and the process flow that the software dictates.

Having the software consultants working with us on the process designs, it should be possible to detect early where the major gaps in the software appear to be occurring. By detecting the gap early, the software vendor can explore the magnitude of the change required to have the software enable the process that we have designed. Also, we can see where we might have to consider alternatives in the Conference Room Pilot.

This was a commendable direction to follow. The Steering Committee took a long-term perspective in making this decision. Their decision was to design the business processes to best meet their requirements. They did not want to give up on seeing what the business should look like just because the current version of the software they had purchased might not support it. The opportunity was there to work with the software vendor and improve the feature/functionality in future releases. The corporation chose to design their supply chain processes and enabling technologies to enhance the competitive edge that they already held in their marketplace. This is a significant lesson that many others, unfortunately, do not follow. Too many organizations let the current versions of systems drive their thinking.

Finding Out More

Is it worth your while to find out more about Process Visualization, Process Culture, and PeopleFlow? It seems the pace of change is not slowing and business process design never stops.

Organizations are continually driven to new and revised business processes in response to the increasing number of stimuli,
including mergers and acquisitions, changing market conditions, demands by customers and suppliers, and the insistence
of the new economy to involve companies in e-business relationships and e-commerce transactions. Other organizations are
simply trying to understand the processes they have today so
that they have a foundation on which to build. If you think that
change will continue to happen within your organization, then
you should find out more about Process Visualization.

Have you been involved in approving the design for a major
business change initiative? What was your experience of the
design process? Were you just given a stack of documents to
read, or was there a design review walk-through? Could you easily follow the gist of the design and role of the technology
enablers? Could you see the integration of business processes, or
did you get the impression that the design had been done in
silos? Perhaps the strategy and business model sounded good to
you at the beginning, but you were left with the sinking feeling
that the design didn't have the strength to lead the organization
towards your intended vision. What would have given you confidence that the business design had the ability to achieve the
anticipated business benefits?

Feeling uneasy at the start of a major business change initiative is uncomfortable. You are fortunate, however, if you
detect this uncertainty at an early stage. Think of the projects
that are right now building and buying technologies, and
modifying systems to implement a design that will never take
their organization towards its vision. You know that once the
spending on technology starts, it can easily accelerate into the
millions. And once it's spent, then what? Even if the systems
provide some new functionality, or the Internet application
impresses you, how often are the business benefits of a major
change initiative fully realized without having solid, integrated processes? Process Visualization can give you a forum to
express your thoughts and reservations about the design, and

specifically point out the areas during the performing of the processes that give you an uneasy feeling. Process Visualization can let you actively participate and express concerns without swamping you with the details of the design.

PART TWO

PeopleFlow—

The Executive Guide to Using Process Visualization

The second part of this book provides an introduction to PeopleFlow. It deals with how to make the concepts of Process Visualization work successfully in your organization.

Chapter 5 discusses the situations *where* PeopleFlow can effectively be used. Supply chains and value chains are primary targets for applying PeopleFlow. Their processes and technologies are constantly changing to meet demands for higher service levels. They demand tight integration for efficient and cost-effective links to work. Value and supply chains are not the only places that organizations can use PeopleFlow to help them with their business process designs.

Chapter 6 explains *what happens* in a project that uses PeopleFlow. It introduces the Business Process Design Project, the recommended first step for your organization to take when you are launching a major business change initiative. Setting the direction for such a project is an essential task for executives. Direction setting discusses the key documents that need to be defined before launching the design team into their work.

Chapter 7 describes *how an executive is involved* in a Business Process Design Project. It describes the role that executives have in the approval of business designs that will have a major impact on their organization.

Chapter 8 explains *what the team does* in a Business Process Design Project. It discusses the team's role during the project and what documentation they develop and deliver. This final chapter describes the style of documentation that forms the foundation for the deliverables of a Business Process Design Project.

CHAPTER FIVE

Where PeopleFlow Can Effectively Be Used

Where to Use PeopleFlow

If you don't get the business process design right at the start, then be prepared to waste time, effort, and resources on systems and technologies that do not deliver what you envisioned. With this in mind, this chapter explains where you can effectively use PeopleFlow and the concepts of Process Visualization. Supply chains and value chains are primary targets for applying these concepts. Their processes and technologies continue to change in an effort to meet the demands for higher customer service levels and operational efficiencies. They demand tight integration to achieve a cost-effective value chain. Operational excellence, the ability to flawlessly execute while adapting to a changing marketplace, continues to be high on the list of executive priorities.

There are two broad reasons that cause organizations to undertake change initiatives: technology and business events in their market and industry.

These were introduced in Chapter 1. This chapter now discusses these situations in more depth, and shows where

PeopleFlow can be used to provide direction to the change initiative.

From a timing perspective, PeopleFlow is ideally used at the start of a business change initiative to guide the Business Process Design Project. This key initial project develops the business process design that will be used as the blueprint for other activities during the implementation. If PeopleFlow was not used at the beginning, it can be used later on to untangle projects that have gone off track. If you find yourself in such a situation, consider using PeopleFlow to get you back on track.

PeopleFlow is scalable; it can be used on large and small projects. Once it becomes an implicit part of your organization's culture, you will find that your people gravitate to using it on projects of all sizes.

Supply Chains and Value Chains

Supply chains and value chains are primary targets for applying PeopleFlow. The movement of products and services through an effective and efficient value chain is a primary target for constant change and improvement. Supply and value chains continue to change today in an effort to meet the demands for higher customer service levels and to gain a competitive advantage through operational efficiencies. Their processes and enabling technologies are critical to keep products and services moving. In the past, the physical aspects of a supply chain received much of the attention, but today they are only one part of the success formula. The people, processes, and information that plan and execute the physical movements are critical to a value chain. The technologies that provide the support to these activities share in the success of achieving exceptional customer service at a competitive price.

Supply and value chains demand tight integration. In order to achieve efficiency and cost-effective operation, all the components involved in forming the chain need to be tightly linked. In an integrated value chain there are many processes happening at the same time. The flow of information is what provides the integration of the various process activities. Sometimes, people need to see information so that they can use it to make decisions and cause activities to start executing. Some information remains inside the systems and is not required until something goes wrong. All the information flows, whether observable or not, are critical to the success of the value chain. Providing the right information at the right time is paramount to orchestrating all the components of planning and executing the activities in a value chain. Without integration, the strength of the chain is diminished and eventually broken.

Operational excellence, the ability to flawlessly execute while adapting to a changing marketplace, continues to be high on the list of an executive's priorities. Making change happen and not missing a beat in your current operations is a goal that needs to be skilfully managed. Making major changes happen seamlessly, so that customers perceive only an increase in your service, is a significant accomplishment. Customers are usually sensitive to your level of service. If you implement a major change and they perceive a drop in service before the expected improvement occurs, the change initiative will probably not have the positive impact that you expected. Flawless execution of a major change requires anticipating what will really happen to the processes, people, and information when you go live with the supporting technologies.

PeopleFlow is at home in the value chain environment. The concepts of Process Visualization have been adapted and applied to supply and value chains, then packaged into the process design toolkit called PeopleFlow. PeopleFlow lets you visualize the changes and their potential impact on your customers. By starting with a design that is well understood by everyone involved, you increase your chances of flawlessly implementing technology and process changes in your value chain.

Change Initiatives Driven by Technology

Nothing moves in a supply and value chain until information flows and processes are enacted. The product or service does not start on its path to the customer until triggered to do so. In most cases this trigger doesn't happen until people and systems have used information to plan and schedule the location and timing of the movements. Then, when the product or service is triggered to move, its movements can be tracked until the customer is satisfied that his or her demands have been met. People, processes, and information all rely on technology to support the activities in a value chain. Today, value chains rely heavily on technology in order to be successful.

The drive to gain a competitive advantage is fuelled by emerging technologies. But technology is changing so rapidly that organizations find it difficult and expensive to constantly keep up with all the advances. Technology applications for value chains continue to be developed because this area offers so much promise. When inventory can be replaced by information, and product movement is reduced through better planning, the drive to employ advanced software and hardware offers the promise of significant savings and better service levels. When an organization starts a change initiative that involves new technologies, they want to be certain that the benefits will be there. They want to know that it will work for their approach to servicing the market. The track record of success shows that just because you choose to implement promising technology advancements doesn't mean you will succeed. But, to not take this road at some time means falling behind your competitors as they seek new ways to define and provide service to your customers.

PeopleFlow can be used for change initiatives where technology is the reason to make changes that will affect your people, processes, and information flows. There are many situations where technology is the driver. These were outlined in Chapter 1 and are used here to discuss their applicability to supply and value chains.

E-business concepts provide the information links to new value chain business models.

The Internet is offering the ability to cost-effectively make information available to all participants throughout a value chain. E-commerce (exchanges and auctions), m-commerce (mobile and wireless), and c-commerce (collaboration) all flood value chain participants with instant information availability. Electronic Data Interchange (EDI) is still used and plays an important role in business transactions. How will the new business models that e-business make possible best be used to leverage your competitive advantage? How will the new enabling technology influence your processes and people? How do you know that your value chain can benefit? PeopleFlow can help you to visualize how e-business can work for your value chain.

Packaged software is pervasive in value chains.

Over the last 15 years, packaged software has dominated in enabling supply chain operations of large and small organizations. Whether the organization is a manufacturer, distributor, or intermediary agent along the chain, most of them continue to implement packaged software to support their mission-critical applications. Applications such as Advanced Planning Systems (APS) and Customer Relationship Management (CRM) are two currently popular supply chain concepts that organizations are buying and implementing. Enterprise Systems (ES) or Enterprise Resource Planning (ERP) systems are still being purchased, implemented, and upgraded. How will the concepts and suggested best practices offered by the upgrades in the software affect your business processes and people? How can you best select these packages and then implement them? PeopleFlow lets you take the concepts and best practices offered by the features and functionality of the software package and integrate them with the rest of your processes and information flows. And it allows you to do this before the software is technically integrated and configured. In fact, by using PeopleFlow, your IT team will be better able to configure and integrate the package with the rest of your enabling technologies. PeopleFlow will also ensure that the team is ready with scenarios and scripts when they start the conference room pilot.

The technology has already been purchased.

Now the task falls to you to implement it successfully! Even though it was not your choice, the challenge is to make it a success. If the fit isn't what you expected, how will you explore how processes can effectively be changed to accommodate the system without negatively impacting the business? How do you recognize when some modifications are necessary? This situation can apply anywhere in an organization and is not specific to value chains. Even if you already own the software, you should still conduct a Business Process Design Project. PeopleFlow can help you discover the true business requirements for you to be successful and competitive in your value chain. There are more options than those contained in the current version of the software. Don't be limited in your designs and thinking by considering only what is in the package.

You have already implemented a premier business system, but you feel your organization is not fully benefiting from the strengths of the technology.

This is a common complaint. You have already made a sizeable investment in new technologies including a premier mission-critical business system to support areas in your supply chain such as your financials, manufacturing, distribution, forecasting and planning, customer service, and marketing operations. You know that this should put you ahead of your competitors. Still, there is a sense among your executive that the organization is not fully benefiting from the potential strength that the new integrated systems and feature-rich functionality provide. This complaint is not limited to any particular application area or software vendor. It doesn't seem to matter if it's your Enterprise System (such as SAP, JD Edwards, Oracle), or your Advanced Planning System (such as i2 Technologies or Manugistics) or your Customer Relationship Management system (such as Siebel, Pivotal, or Saratoga). Executives commonly feel that they should be able to further leverage the substantial investment in their current technologies. Is it the system's functionality, your people's understanding, or your processes that need to be examined and re-aligned?

Change Initiatives Driven by Business Events

Change does not only depend on a new technology. There are many change drivers within your industry and the marketplace can cause you to look at how people, process, and technology might be changed to enhance your competitive position. Often, events occur inside your organization that make you launch major business change initiatives.

Customers and suppliers are pushing you.

Your external stakeholders want to form tighter relationships with you. Your customers and suppliers want you to become more involved, effective, and integrated with their supply chain processes and systems. Customers want you to take responsibility further into their organizations for your products and services. Suppliers want to get further into your organization to help manage the smooth replenishment of their products. The word "collaboration" continues to be mentioned as the type of partnering relationship that will make the supply chain more effective. A strong mutual trust in the relationship is needed to make these proposed partnerships work. The executive wants to understand the benefits and risks. The concepts sound interesting to you, but do you understand how it will all work? How will the new relationship really benefit your organization? You need to understand how business processes will work in these proposed closer relationships before taking the next steps and committing to a pilot. Seeing how the End-to-End processes will flow through multiple organizations and be improved by the new concept is critical to moving forward. PeopleFlow offers a low-risk project in which all the involved organizations can participate. By gaining an understanding together of how the proposed relationship will work, the sense of trust grows between everyone involved. PeopleFlow can give confidence and understanding to move forward into an operational pilot.

You are about to outsource part of your operations.

Outsourcing parts of a supply chain to a third-party logistics (3PL) provider is a common occurrence today as organizations move to retain only their core competencies. 3PL firms are thriving as this global trend continues. It could be your physical supply chain warehousing and transportation operations, or customer service and accounts receivable, or procurement and payables that you are looking to outsource. You want to ensure that each organization understands the other's responsibilities. You need to have all key activities, especially those involving customers, continue in a seamless manner and ensure that nothing falls between the cracks. By outsourcing, there will now be two organizations that have touch points with your customers, you, and your 3PL. The integration between your two organizations needs to be very well defined and visible, so that all systems and manual processes are apparent to the teams from both organizations as they implement the transition to a new relationship. How will you ensure that the people, processes, and technologies from both organizations align to enhance service to customers? It isn't just a matter of making sure that the EDI transactions flow smoothly between both organizations. You need to see how the processes are going to operate and ensure that both organizations are aligned to provide enhanced service to customers from day one. Defining and documenting the new relationship in an effective manner is imperative to the success of the implementation project and to the building of a strong and trusting working partnership.

The explosive growth in your organization is overwhelming your resources.

Before the current high level of customer service starts to fail, you need to relieve the pressure on the organization. It's obvious that you do not have the horsepower to go much further. Your best people are stretched and your success may soon lead to failure. You can sense that your level of customer service excellence will start to fail if you don't react now. But what needs to be fixed? Does the answer lie in more people, improved business processes, or better technology support? PeopleFlow can help you spot your bottlenecks and eliminate them. It can help you re-align processes so that your people can more effectively be used to service customers. Before you hire more people or investigate new systems, make sure you understand where the problems lie.

You are working through a merger.

Both organizations have their own systems and business processes, but now you need to put the organizations together. You want to ensure that each organization understands the other. What are the strengths and weaknesses of both organizations' systems and processes? What are the differences and why do they exist? Where can innovation be leveraged? How can the best of both worlds be merged so that the systems and processes together form a whole that is stronger than its parts? PeopleFlow offers a neutral environment where the best of both organizations can be openly viewed and explored.

Continuous improvement programs give you benefits of ongoing incremental changes.

Your continuous improvement program has produced some impressive results to date. You know that by continuously refining your processes and systems, you can benefit from ongoing incremental change. Using PeopleFlow on a continuous basis can ensure that your people are prepared to participate when a major change initiative starts.

You need to look at the effectiveness of your processes, people, and supporting technology.

Something appears to be out of line within your operations. You are suspicious that the ratio of expenses to sales is higher than your competitors, yet everyone in your organization seems busy. You may not want to call it re-engineering, because of the negative connotations of the term. But, you need to do something that objectively investigates where the problem lies. Is it the systems, the business processes, or the people that are failing to make you more productive?

Projects That Go Off Track

What if you already started a change initiative and see that it has gone off track? No matter what driver started your business change initiative, your initiative appears to have gone off track. Even though you did not use PeopleFlow at the start, it's not too late to bring it into the project now. The situations described below range from the ideal to disastrous. Even the worst situation can be salvaged, and the damage to staff morale and business practices can be turned around. PeopleFlow can provide an important tool with which you can turn the situation around.

The Ideal Situation

• Your organization wants to start a business change initiative that involves implementing new technology. It hasn't selected or purchased any technology yet.

• You know that your first step is to understand your business processes.

• You start with your business objectives, work to determine your business requirements, and then design your business processes. Throughout these steps you determine the requirements that the technology must be capable of supporting.

• Now you can start the search for the best technology and implementation partner.

• You select and purchase the systems that best fit your technology requirements and business processes. Your teams are ready to start the implementation.

• The executive has the confidence to launch the technology implementation, and they understand what the end result will look like.

• You know that business and technical issues will arise throughout the implementation, but you expect no big surprises or showstoppers.

PeopleFlow is useful in this scenario right from the very start. PeopleFlow's role is to start your team off in the right direction and keep it driving to a successful business process design that can be wholeheartedly approved by your executive group before proceeding with the technology selection and implementation.

By fulfilling this role, PeopleFlow creates a strong platform from which your organization can tackle the technology-selection process. You will find that your organization will be in the driver's seat during the selection and purchase of the technology. You will be better able to direct technology vendors in developing custom demonstrations specifically dealing with your business processes. You will be able to move beyond the vendors' standard sales demos. Your team will have the scripts and the process flows for the business processes that you want to enable with the new technology. You will be able to see how the vendors' technology performs against your business process requirements. And finally, you will have a knowledgeable and confident team that knows what they are looking to buy.

Soon after acquiring your new systems, a typical implementation plan from a software package vendor will call for a conference room pilot (also called a solution design workshop). This pilot is intended to let you discover how the software package can best be configured to support your business processes. The output from your Business Process Design Project is the major input to this pilot. Your teams will have defined all the critical business scenarios as well as have designed the process flows. These now become invaluable as the starting point for the work in the pilot. The major difference between the PeopleFlow performance that you saw to approve the design and the pilot is: now more of the actual technology is being used to enable the processes. Without the PeopleFlow documentation as input, your team will have to develop it now, before the conference room pilot can begin. But because you have followed the ideal path, the pilot gets off to a quick start.

The Less-Than-Ideal Situation

- Your organization gets excited and perhaps over-confident about a new technology and goes straight out and buys it after only a brief demo.

- Now you need to implement it. You're not happy with the talk about modifications.

Even if you have already selected your technology, People-Flow can help. It's fortunate that your organization realizes that business processes are important and need to be considered before the software is implemented. You may feel that this situation is very far from the ideal situation, but the steps still need to be the same. You can still use PeopleFlow to effectively drive your Business Process Design Project. The team needs clear direction and criteria as they learn about and consider the strengths and weaknesses of the technology's functionality. They need to know how to proceed when they find gaps. You need to decide where you can change your business process to fit the software and where it is absolutely necessary to modify the software to support your process. PeopleFlow gives you the ability to explore these options and examine their impact on your value chain.

Approaching the Edge

- You acquire the new technology first.

- You believe that the best way to implement is to get right into the conference room pilot and see how the software can run your business.

- It all seems a good idea at the time. But several months into the project, the team is going around in circles, and everyone is at each other's throat. They can't even agree on what "run the business" means.

- You dig into the project and discover some interesting problems:

  a. Nobody can agree on how the business should work, let alone how the software can run the business.

  b. Your team has mixed feelings and differing opinions about how the business currently works.

c. You find a fundamental lack of alignment amongst the team members.

d. Someone points out to you that policies are often ignored and that exceptions have become the norm. Processes are conducted in ways that everyone knows are wrong, but that have become the modus operandi.

e. The team is struggling to see how their wish list could be implemented using the new software.

f. The confidence, direction, and authority to complete the project are fading among the executive. They want to withdraw their resources from the project.

It's not too late to take action and get this project moving forward again. Although you have lost time, resources, and some credibility, PeopleFlow can turn those negatives around. The first thing to do is to stop the conference room pilot. Back up, admit the false start, then use PeopleFlow to get your team moving forward on a Business Process Design Project.

The Catastrophe That Can Be Turned Around

- You've been involved in a technology-driven project for almost a year now.

- The program did not include a Business Process Design Project. The feature/functionality of the new technology is driving the implementation without regard for an approved business process design. As in the previous scenario, the team could not agree on what "run the business" means and have little alignment amongst themselves.

- Millions of dollars have already been spent on technology, consultants, and internal resources. There's nothing tangible to show for it. The witch-hunt is gathering momentum, and heads are about to roll.

- Instead of abandoning the project, you want to salvage what has been done and get back on track. You know it would be better to completely switch tracks and start again with a process-driven project. But this will take some selling to the rest of the executive. You have gone well beyond simply backing up and admitting a false start. Now, you have to convince a number of sceptical people that it's worthwhile to keep going and that this time around the implementation approach will lead to success.

- You think that your salvaging efforts might pay off if you can successfully redirect the focus towards the business processes. A lot of good work has already been done and will prove useful.

It's never too late to take corrective action, but organizations do reach a point where simply abandoning a project is easier than the effort to turn it around. In this catastrophe scenario, most of the executive probably want to bail out and save face as best they can rather than try to get the project moving forward again. The first thing you need to do is slow down to a snail's pace the technology development or modification that's currently happening. You need to buy some time and curtail the spending.

Even though PeopleFlow delivers a process design that can be understood and approved by the executive before the design is implemented, you are going to have a hard sell to convince anyone to start over again. In this situation, you do not have the time for the normal flow of events in a Business Process Design Project. Your best tack to get the project back on track lies in convincing the rest of the executive that PeopleFlow is capable of rapid deployment by people who have used it before in difficult situations. You need to bring in people trained on PeopleFlow to work as a shadow team and rapidly get you to a business process design that can direct the implementation project. The Business Process Design Project can be modified to look more like a conference room pilot, especially if any of the newly developed or purchased systems are capable of being used by the team. The foundation concepts of PeopleFlow can support the teams in working together in the same direction. Because time is of the essence in this difficult scenario, the PeopleFlow style of performing the business processes can be supplemented by using parts of the new enabling technologies. This combination of performing the processes and using the technology where possible will help you to see where the gaps, issues, and problems really lie.

PeopleFlow Is Scalable

PeopleFlow can be used on any size of project. It is designed to support large organizations during major business change initiatives. It can be used where projects are big and involve a large number of people and processes. It's an important tool where the scope and complexity of a project will have a major impact on an organization.

PeopleFlow can be equally effective when the project or its scope is small. You don't have to have large teams working for months on design work to use this proven methodology. Whenever business processes are involved in a project, PeopleFlow can assist a team to achieve more comprehensive designs in less time.

A Business Process Design Project doesn't have to be big, but it does have to happen. You do have to go through the steps to reap the full benefits. The design must be documented and approved. PeopleFlow's techniques can be used just as effectively to document a smaller stand-alone process as it can a large integrated project. Obtaining approval for the design doesn't have to be part of a gala performance of process-flow scenarios. It can be a simple walk-through with the executives who will be impacted by the process. PeopleFlow works for simple processes in large organizations and for a large number of integrated processes in smaller organizations as well as for large-scale integrated processes. PeopleFlow is scalable.

What Happens in a PeopleFlow-Driven Project?

Activities in a Business Process Design Project

The typical steps in a Business Process Design Project are illustrated in Diagram 6.1. This diagram illustrates *what happens* in a design project. Remember that PeopleFlow is scalable and can be adapted to fit any size of design project. This book is an executive guide and does not touch on the *how-to-make-it-happen* aspects of PeopleFlow. That topic is fully covered in the PeopleFlow practitioner's guide, entitled *PeopleFlow—a Handbook for Crafting Business Processes*. More information on the practitioner's guide can be found in Appendix A, page 161.

Get Organized and Launch

Unfortunately, many programs and projects are launched by just throwing the designated participants into the deep end and hoping for the best. This leaves the team floundering and unable to bring about change. They often fail to produce results and the expected benefits. Getting organized for a major business change initiative should be treated as a project unto itself. In order to structure your thinking and lexicon, think of the overall effort of the change initiative as "the program" and all the components that make it up as "the projects."

PeopleFlow does not attempt to address all the tasks that program and project managers need to accomplish, or the political challenges that need to be met before a program for a major business change is launched. There are a few key topics, however, that will be discussed.

Clearly Define the Program

The first task is to very clearly define what the program is all about. Governance, scope, and organization are all critical to clarity. For a major business change initiative, it is imperative to develop a comprehensive Program Charter. This charter is essential in defining the overall program for the organization. The following are significant sections of the Program Charter that are key:

- Business Objectives
- Program Objectives
- Program Scope
- Program Organization

The program organization needs to be headed by a Steering Committee composed of the Executive Sponsor and all other executives impacted by the scope of the program. These terms are further explained in the Glossary of Terms in Appendix B on page 165.

Clearly Define the Business Process Design Project

Since the Business Process Design Project is the first project in the program, it needs to be structured as soon as the program is clearly defined. Like the Program Charter, the Project Charter is essential in defining this first project for the organiza-

Diagram 6.1 What Happens in a PeopleFlow-driven Design Project

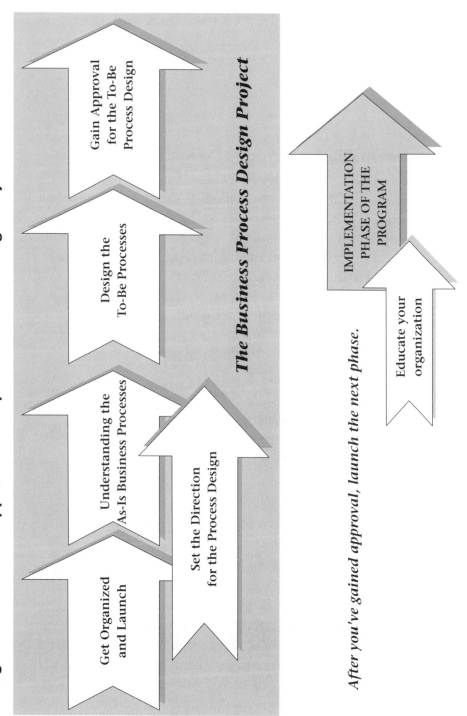

Get Organized
and Launch

Understanding the
As-Is Business Processes

Set the Direction
for the Process Design

Design the
To-Be Processes

Gain Approval
for the To-Be
Process Design

The Business Process Design Project

After you've gained approval, launch the next phase.

IMPLEMENTATION
PHASE OF THE
PROGRAM

Educate your
organization

tion. The following are significant sections of the Project Charter that are key:

- Project Objectives
- Project Scope
- Project Organization

Select the Business Process Design Team

The Business Process Design Project is due to start after the kick-off. First it needs to be staffed. Selecting the right people for the various roles is essential to the success of the project. In the PeopleFlow practitioner's guide, the roles and skills required to properly staff the business process design team are discussed in further detail. For now, it's important to realize that a mixture of skills and people from the business side and from the information technology group is a must. Here's a list of the positions required to staff a project. On smaller projects some of these positions and functions can be combined.

- Project Manager
- Process Team Leaders
- Integration Team Leader
- Business Process Analysts
- Information Technology Analysts
- Subject Matter Experts

Introduce the Business Change Initiative to the Entire Organization

It's important to properly launch a major new change initiative within your organization because it will have a profound impact on the organization for a significant length of time. The introduction needs to reach everyone. The change initiative can be introduced in a variety of ways, including face-to-face meetings or video presentations on your organization's Intranet site. Make this launch as personable as possible and do not just leave a voice-mail, e-mail, or written document announcing the program's launch. The presentation should start with the CEO or Steering Committee Chairperson introducing the program. Other key players can take on the task of informing the audience about the objectives, scope, organization, communication, and timelines for the program. The presentation should set the right tone. People have to understand why it's important, what will be happening, when it will be completed, what is their role, and what parts of the organization will be most impacted by this business change initiative.

Kick-off the Business Process Design Project

The project kick-off is held for the direct benefit of the members of the design team. The agenda is focused on introducing more details about how the program and the project will operate. The kick-off explains specifically how the Business Process Design Project will be organized and conducted, what needs to be accomplished, and when. At the end of the session, the team should feel that they know where the project is headed, what each person's role is on the team, and what are the immediate next steps. This kick-off is a comprehensive session as this typical agenda for the meeting shows:

- Introduction by Program Director/Manager
- Program Objectives
- Project Charter
  - Purpose of this Project Charter
  - Project Background
  - Project Objectives
  - Project Scope
  - Project Organization
  - Timeline for the design
  - Project Timetable
  - Project Strategies
  - Project Deliverables
  - Quality Assurance
  - Assumptions and Constraints

- Status Meetings and Communications
- Program Management Office Procedures
  ○ Project Issues Management
  ○ Change Control
  ○ Approvals
- Design Principles
- Top-Down Project Plan
- The next steps—Team Training and Certification
- Making a start on As-Is Business Processes

The project kick-off is a roll-up-the-sleeves-and-let's-start style of meeting. Gauge how the newly formed team feels at the end of the sessions and in discussions with individuals afterwards. It's important that the team knows its direction and what is expected of it.

Train and Certify the Team

Training and certification ensure that the team is ready to start working. You will need to conduct a number of sessions that train and certify the team members in the PeopleFlow techniques and tools that they will use during the process design project. These training sessions should not be onerous, but they need to be thorough and filled with enough exercises so that the techniques can be grasped. A prerequisite is that all team members know the basics of the software-drawing package that will be used throughout the program. Topics covered during training and certification include:

Process Thinking—Understanding the Concepts of Process Visualization and PeopleFlow

- PeopleFlow in its design, approval, and educational modes
- Building blocks and components of a business process
- Levels of detail in business processes and the Top-Down approach to the design process
- Types of charts that will be used to document the business processes

- Creating and drawing process charts
- Documentation formats and templates
- Scenarios
- Business rules and algorithms
- Decision tables and use-cases

Participative Theatre
- Performing business processes—acting out the different parts in a process

The PeopleFlow Game
- Conducting a mini Business Process Design Project

PeopleFlow Certification
- Demonstrating and evaluating individuals' competence with PeopleFlow techniques

Initial Planning for the Upcoming Project
- Roles and expectations of the team members
- Project plans and timelines
- Work patterns

Training takes approximately one week, depending on the size of the team and the magnitude of the initial Business Process Design Project. Some organizations like to divide the training into shorter sessions spread over two weeks. This gives their teams a better chance to digest all the new information and prepare for their certification. Don't cut corners with the team's training; this investment in people's time will pay off on the first project.

Certification allows team members to show that they are ready to meet project expectations. The team members and the Steering Committee want to know that each person can be relied on to do his or her part in creating and documenting the best business process design possible. After training is completed, certification of the individual team members is highly encouraged and recommended. If some members are not capable of participating and contributing to this fast-paced project, it's best that everyone involved knows this upfront. Certification allows team members to challenge themselves and show their level of competence in using the PeopleFlow techniques. Do not assume that just because people have taken the training classes, they are capable of producing consistent documentation and can think and design in a process manner. Certification testing takes one day to complete and gives each person an assessment of his or her current level of strengths and weaknesses in understanding and using process design techniques.

Set the Direction for the Business Process Design

Setting a clear course of direction for the design team is the first place that the executive can have a significant impact on the success of the Business Process Design Project. During the initial step of "Get organized and launched," the executive develops documentation for both the program and the Business Process Design Project, including the business objectives, program objectives and scope, and project objectives and scope. These statements provide the design team and the organization with a high-level view of the stated direction of both the business and the program. That initial level of direction setting is both important and necessary, but the design team also needs precise direction and specific details to set the direction for their Business Process Design Project. Because this is the initial project of the program, it's imperative that this design project is directed in a way that is easily understood by everyone. Meeting the timeline and budget for the project is directly related to establishing and conveying a well-defined sense of direction from the beginning.

The next level of direction-setting documents developed by the executive will describe how narrow or broad a view the design team should take during the Business Process Design Project. Are they to explore innovative ideas and unproven technologies, or are they to stay within more conventional boundaries? Does the executive have clear and specific requirements, or is this project an opportunity to explore and develop requirements together? What is known and needed, and what requires further investigation and analysis?

There are four specific direction-setting documents for the executive to establish:

1. Business Requirements Repository—requirements needed to achieve your Business Objectives

2. Business Policies Repository—current, proposed, and potential areas for change

3. Statement of Direction on External and Internal Influences

4. Design Principles

Business Requirements Repository

This repository is a collection of the business requirements that will be met by the business process design. A Business Requirement is a statement about how the organization needs to operate to successfully achieve its business objectives. A requirement specifies what the executive wish to have and what they thinks they need to have in order to accomplish their business objectives. Requirements sometimes refer to a best practice or a technology that needs to be implemented. See the Glossary of Terms in Appendix B on page 165 for further discussion and examples of Business Requirements.

Business requirements are direction setting because they emphatically state the specifications that the design needs to achieve in order to be successful. They *set the bar* and express in business terminology what senior executives are looking for. The requirements become the criteria that the design needs to meet in order to gain approval. They also give the process teams, who are working on various aspects of the design, a consistent set of specifications that assist in achieving an integrated design. The requirement statements can prevent a design team from going off on a tangent.

Although not all the business requirements will be known at

this point, usually an initial list can be developed at this early stage in the project. The list will continue to grow and change; that is the nature of the design process. However, initial thinking on business requirements is important to provide direction to the team in the direction-setting session. The PeopleFlow practitioner's guide goes into the details of setting up and maintaining a Business Requirements Repository.

Business Policy Repository

This repository is a collection of the business policies that are required to govern the business process design. A Business Policy is a statement that directs the appropriate behaviours for an organization to follow when dealing with the activities and actions of internal people, external people, systems, and other organizations such as customers and suppliers. A policy is a summary statement about the course of action that the organization has chosen to follow in a given circumstance. A policy is used to guide decisions and resolve conflicts. See the Glossary of Terms in Appendix B on page 165 for further discussion and examples of Business Policies.

Not all of the new policies will be known at this stage of the project. But this is a good opportunity to document the policies that are known to impact the business processes within the scope of this project. You can start thinking about new and existing policies that will need to be changed. This initial thinking is required for the team's direction-setting review; it will give them a sense of how the executive is thinking about policy direction. The PeopleFlow practitioner's guide goes into the details of setting up and maintaining a Business Policy Repository.

Statement of Direction on External and Internal Influences

This document defines the "scope for innovation" that the

Steering Committee will accept into the project at this time. The executives on the Steering Committee, including the CIO, develop the Statement of Direction. Its purpose is to direct the team's thinking and activities by attempting to set boundaries regarding what innovations in technologies and processes should be considered. The document is not meant to stifle innovation, but rather is an attempt to focus attention on the scope and possibly the budget of the project. For instance, if your project is meant to be a wide-open, check-out-every-possibility style of project in which to explore innovative solutions, then you should clearly state that. The Statement of Direction may also contain options and choices that need further consideration before the executive can make a decision and set a clear direction. The executive states the options and choices in order to challenge the team to analyze, and recommend back to the Steering Committee, the best direction to follow. Diagram 6.2 depicts the influences that need to be considered in the Statement of Direction.

Nothing causes more confusion and wastes more time than letting a design team start off on a Business Process Design Project without an understanding of the degree of freedom as well as the boundaries and constraints within which the Steering Committee wants them to work. Organizations want to encourage creativity and new ideas in business processes and enablers. Nobody wants to reject or discourage use of technologies that can be beneficial to efficiency, effectiveness, and competitiveness. However, there are limits to the time and resources that can be expended on a project before results are expected and business benefits achieved. It is the responsibility of the Steering Committee to set the direction and limits on where originality is required versus where it is best to adopt industry standards and best practices. Developing the Statement of Direction is explained in the PeopleFlow practitioner's guide.

Diagram 6.2 Influences that impact the Business Process Design Project as well as the technology implementation projects

INITIAL THOUGHTS ABOUT OUR SYSTEM AND TECHNOLOGY DIRECTION
- Current thinking about how to enable the business processes
- Involvement of Legacy systems

BUSINESS DEMANDS BY OUR CUSTOMERS AND SUPPLIERS
- Pressures for new business relationships and technologies to make the industry more effective

DIRECTIONS OF OUR INDUSTRY AND COMPETITORS
- Emerging directions and relationships in our industry

NEW AND UNPROVEN CONCEPTS; LATEST THINKING IN THE LITERATURE
- New ideas that present the chance to achieve competitive advantage if they can be successfully implemented and

OUR DIRECTION-SETTING DOCUMENTS
- Business Objectives
- Program Objectives
- Business Requirements
- Business Policies

INDUSTRY BEST PRACTICES
- Proven business processes
- Standard practices demonstrated to achieve efficiencies

INDUSTRY STANDARDS IN TECHNOLOGY
- Protocols and Standards such as EDI transactions and Serialized Shipping Container Code (SSCC#)

EMERGING TECHNOLOGIES
- Industry Exchanges using Internet technologies
- Wireless devices and applications

PACKAGED SOFTWARE
- Integrated ERP packages
- Best-of-Breed application packages
(These solutions are readily available even though they may not exactly support our

BUSINESS PROCESS DESIGN PROJECT AND TECHNOLOGY IMPLEMENTATION PROJECTS

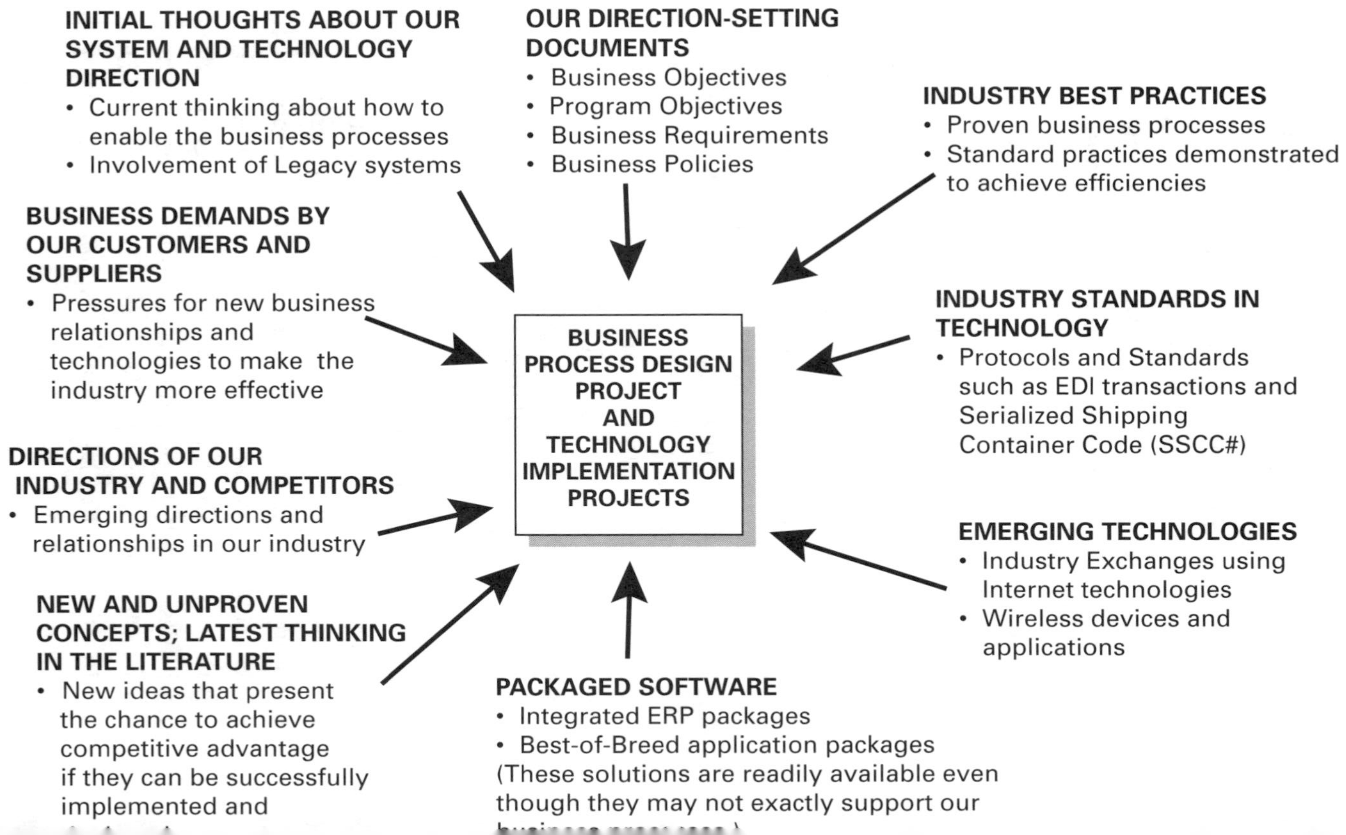

Design Principles

Design Principles are statements about the fundamental approaches or foundations that the program will endeavour to use as the basis for the design. Design Principles are those high-level statements that the design team will strive to meet. They are ideals, and if they can be achieved or even approached, then the likelihood of achieving an inspired design is increased. Some people call these "motherhood and apple pie" statements and do not want to bother with them. But design principles can be very useful during the project because they can act as a sounding board against which to test a design or design alternatives. Design Principles endure throughout the program, whereas the business requirements are often changed and enhanced. So when the design team or the Steering Committee are faced with making a decision on which way to proceed, having fundamental principles to test the design against can be a logical lifesaver. See the Glossary of Terms in Appendix B on page 165 for further discussion and examples of Design Principles.

Direction-Setting Documents

A review of the direction-setting documents starts the team working in the right direction. After the team training and certification, you will want to get the team working on the project as quickly as possible. Do not start them into the work just yet. A review session is needed to get all team members "level-set" on the direction-setting documents that the executive has been developing. Executives on the Steering Committee are encouraged to attend the session with the team so that the two groups have a clear understanding of the expectations of each other and of the deliverables that the design project will produce. Review of the direction-setting documents includes:

- Initial cut of the Business Requirements Repository
- Initial cut of the Business Policies Repository
- Statement of Direction on External and Internal Influences
- Design Principles

All of the work that you have done to prepare the direction-setting documents comes to fruition here. The goal of this session is to make sure the design team clearly understands where the Steering Committee wants this project to go, and what boundaries the team is being asked to respect. Even though the Process Team Leaders assisted the Steering Committee in preparing some of the material, it is very important that everyone goes through this session together and participates in the discussions. The session is successful if the team leaves the meeting with a solid understanding of the direction. Not everyone may agree with some directions, but at least they will understand why the Steering Committee has chosen them. The Program Manager or a facilitator chairs this session so that all executives can participate in the discussions.

Most organizations tend to skip over the direction-setting activities in the rush to get things going. Make the effort to define the direction for your Business Process Design Project, and you will find that it has a better chance of proceeding faster and more smoothly. The team will have a better understanding of the vision they have been asked to deliver.

Understand the As-Is Business Processes

The design team's first assignment is to document and validate the business processes as they currently exist and operate. This step ensures that the team members will all have the same understanding of today's processes and business rules. Documenting the As-Is business processes is often a thankless task since the real focus of the project is to get on with the new To-Be designs. But doing a good job at this stage can save hours of work and research later. Not everything in the To-Be design will be different from the current state. For this reason alone the As-Is is worth doing right. For those parts of the processes that will remain the same, the As-Is documentation will simply be copied into the To-Be design. The As-Is can be a good place for the newly trained design team to try out and perfect their documentation skills before the project starts on the To-Be design. You may be surprised at how misunderstood the current business processes are in your organization and at the lack of agreement on how things work today.

As-Is documentation consists of the following deliverables:

- End-to-End As-Is business process charts and narratives
- Detailed charts and narratives for specific As-Is processes, especially if they have the possibility of remaining relatively unchanged in the To-Be design
- Current business rules and algorithms used in the business processes
- Scenarios and situations that the processes are capable of handling today
- As-Is Process Analysis chart showing the strengths/weaknesses of the current processes

Unless your current processes are already well documented, you should spend the time and effort to complete this key step. If you find that your current processes are well documented, do not recast them into a PeopleFlow documentation style. If your organization is like most, you will find only a partially complete set of As-Is documentation. In this case, ask the team to validate that the documents accurately reflect what is happening today, and add to them as needed to make them complete.

Design the To-Be Business Processes

Finally, the work to design and document the new business processes can start! All the work leading up to this point will prove itself worthwhile as the team gets into the To-Be design.

PeopleFlow uses a Top-Down design approach to develop the To-Be business process design. Starting from a high-level viewpoint of the business processes, the design is expanded down into the layers of detail. To see examples of the documentation and charts, refer to Appendix D, Examples of PeopleFlow Documentation on page 181.

As the design project goes into high gear, you can observe the project and see these activities:

- The Process Team Leaders start the design work by outlining the high-level processes of the To-Be design.

- In a large project, the processes are organized into chunks of work, and work packages are defined and launched.

- End-to-End process flows are designed to handle the key business scenarios. Team members from each of the process teams perform them, as the details are refined.

- Each team develops its own detailed charts that show mainline paths, resolutions, and exceptions. The process teams perform their processes and explore options to enable them.

- The Integration Team works behind the scenes to ensure that the design stays tied together. Processes, data flows, and timelines of events all need to stay integrated as the level of detail of the design goes deeper. Integration meetings ensure that all teams keep pulling in the same direction.

- The IT representatives participate on the teams as the process design unfolds. They advise where technology enablers can be employed to support the business processes. They also provide the rest of the team with expertise and guidance so that the other team members do not drift off on a technology tangent. Initial thinking about technology enablers starts to appear on the process charts.

The To-Be Design

The To-Be design is at the heart of the Business Process Design Project. PeopleFlow provides the structure to support the development and documentation of the new process design. It also encourages creativity as the team works through the details. The team follows the Top-Down Approach to working through the levels of detail in the business process design. The Process Team Leaders first set the design framework by developing the high-level charts. The teams then start to refine the process flows for their particular business processes. End-to-End processes are developed to support business scenarios. The team members become actors and play the parts of the business processes in Participative Theatre sessions. They pass information between themselves as they act out what the process is doing and why. Other team members note changes that need to be made on their process charts and capture issues and gaps that need to be resolved so the design can proceed. The Integration Team notes changes and additions that have been agreed to for the End-to-End processes. All team members are involved in the Participative Theatre sessions. Everyone needs to understand the structure of the design at this stage.

The design and development of detailed-level processes is where teams usually excel. This is where the innovation really starts to appear—it's an exciting part of the project. Now the teams are working at a level of detail at which it seems more natural to think and work. This is the level where observable tasks occur and the components of enabling technologies are more directly linked to the tasks. Initially, the design team may want to jump to this level of detail. You need to ensure that the teams go through the layers of detail so that the design is controlled, and key areas are not missed in the rush to apply the latest technology. It's critical to use the Statement of Direction on External and Internal Influences to keep the thinking within the boundaries defined by the Steering Committee. It's important to show the current and proposed enabling technologies on the detailed level charts. This is where the team uses all their training and know-how to design and fully document the business processes for your organization's future.

The Integration Team

Keeping it all tied together is the job of the Integration Team. In order to keep the design integrated, the End-to-End processes are used to keep the process teams all pulling in the same direction. The Integration Team takes on a significant role in directing the PeopleFlow sessions during the Integration Meetings. The details of the design always need to be tested to ensure that the entire design remains integrated.

IT's Critical Role

IT has the critical role of enabling the processes with the right technologies. It is really at the detailed level that a lot of the decisions are made as to how the design will actually look and how it will be enabled using various technologies. It may sound easy to start selecting technology enablers, but getting there takes a number of facilitated sessions and many hours of "what if?" analysis with the business members on the team working closely with the IT representatives. At this point in the project, the team makes decisions about which types of technology to propose to enable the process design. The Statement of Direction can take on a key role now in deciding which technology direction to follow. This stage of the project is not a selection of a specific vendor's technology. Ideally, the technology selection step will happen after the Business Process Design Project.

Taking the Show on the Road

The team decides when the business process design is ready to be shown to a wider audience—the executive and key stakeholders. When the design team feels that they have enough confidence in their proposed design to present it to the key stakeholders and executive, then the initial round of gaining approval for the design can begin. The executive sponsor will have already seen some of the design and should advise the team about their degree of readiness.

Gain Approval for the Proposed Business Processes

It's show time! Time to perform the business process design for the executive and key stakeholders and show them how the concepts and newly proposed process design work all comes together. An approval is needed to take the business process design out of this design project and into the next phase of the change initiative, which involves the technology implementation. But before the executive and key stakeholders give their approval, there will be a lot of questions and discussions about the processes, concepts, policies, business rules, and enabling systems. The performance is the catalyst that makes the business process design explicit and actively engages the stakeholders. The team should expect some rework. Remember that the audience in this play can, and usually will, question the "script"—and even ask for it to be changed. If significant rethinking and rework is required, the executive may request another performance of the scenarios. But, in the end, gaining approval is a very satisfying process for everyone. The team should be proud that their audience now understands the subtleties and creativity of their design. The executive should emerge confident that they have a design and a team that has proven itself worthy of continuing investment. Here are the steps to gaining approval:

1. Prepare for the performance

The team chooses a few key scenarios that will show the essence of all their work. Like professional actors, they rehearse the scenarios diligently so that the executive can walk into the performance and watch as their business processes come to life. Nothing new has to be developed here; however, the performances of the selected business processes need to be fine-tuned so that the pace is steady and holds the audience's attention.

2. Deliver the performance

The actors do a marvellous job as they perform the different scenarios. There is usually only praise from the audience for their efforts in helping provide insight into often vague business process activities and system enablers. But there's a serious side to the performance as well that can result in the team being sent back to rework the design, and then schedule another performance. The audience may have issues that need to be resolved. They may not like how the design is supporting part of a process, or they may not think that it fully supports the Business Requirement. It may be necessary to rethink a policy and associated business rules at the Steering Committee level and then give this back to the team to redesign. The initial direction given to the team may be seen to cause too much complexity and information churn to support what was, at first, thought to be a simple process. These are healthy discussions. PeopleFlow can help to give senior executives the ability to observe and understand the impact on the business of their direction-setting policy and business requirement statements. If some rework is required at this point, it's usually small in the overall scheme of the entire change initiative.

Remember—if you do not feel convinced that you have achieved the right foundation for the business process design at this point in the program, do not let the program go on to the next stage. Spend the time now to get it right.

3. Rework the design, if necessary

The team takes the processes and the issues that the stakeholders have determined need more design work, and reworks them. The executive may need to spend some time in rework themselves to clarify direction, policies, or business requirements. When ready, the team will give another performance to demonstrate the revised thinking. This is an iterative process and will continue until final approval is gained. The Business Process Design Project is completed!

Educate Your Organization

The business process design has been approved, the team has completed the Business Process Design Project, and the technology implementation phase has just been launched. The design team and an expanded IT team want to move ahead. The people responsible for change management will want to focus their attention on educating the rest of the organization and bringing them up to speed on key aspects of the approved business process design. PeopleFlow can assist the change management effort to alleviate the fear of the unknown that commonly exists among people not directly involved in a project. PeopleFlow can effectively unveil the new business process design and directions to a wider audience. You need to make the business processes come alive once again, and give people a first look at their future. This is key, as their jobs may be highly impacted by the new process designs. Here is how PeopleFlow can assist in your change management activities:

1. Review the business drivers

Review of the Business Objectives, Business Requirements, Policies, and Design Concepts to introduce what needs to be achieved and why. Because some people may not have attended the introductory meeting to the business change initiative, it's important that they gain an appreciation for the program. This can be achieved by walking them through the main drivers as well as the concepts behind the design. If you do not first introduce the drivers and concepts, you will find that people are not ready for the performances.

2. Hold educational performances

The scripts have all been prepared by the design team, so the show is ready to be taken on the road. This time it will be performed for an audience that is very aware of what is happening today but has had little exposure to the thinking of the design team. They will have many questions and concerns. Be sure to have your change management professionals on hand to answer people's questions about what will happen to them. The design team will be involved with the next step in the program, so they may not have the time to conduct repeated performances of the scenarios. To effectively educate your organization, you will more than likely require a number of performances, often in wide-ranging geographic locations. Here are some options to consider when planning the education performances:

- Rotate members of the design team throughout the education performances.
- Use subject matter experts, who helped during the design, as actors. Rotate them in with other team members.
- Videotape the original cast of actors as they perform the scenarios; then use the tapes for education sessions. Consider having one or more team members present when showing the video to answer design questions and provide commentary to the audience in order to make the presentation more personable.

CHAPTER SEVEN

❦

The Executive's Role in PeopleFlow

Executives can take on one or more of the following roles during the Business Process Design Project and for the duration of the business change initiative. For smaller projects the roles may be combined into one person. In this chapter, the roles of the following executives are discussed:

- Executive Sponsor

- Steering Committee Chairperson

- Steering Committee Member

- Program Director/Manager

The best way to start to appreciate your role as an executive is to look at an overview of the areas where you need to be involved. The major activities of a Business Process Design Project were summarized at the beginning of the last chapter. Using these same activities, the executive's involvement and role is summarized beside each of the project's activities in the table below. If you are the Executive Sponsor of the Business Process Design Project, then your role is expanded further than that described below.

Executive Roles in a Business Process Design Project

	Executive Involvement	Executive Role

GET ORGANIZED AND LAUNCH

Clearly define the program.	MAJOR	CONTRIBUTOR and APPROVER
Clearly define the Business Process Design Project.	MAJOR	APPROVER
Select the business process design team.	MAJOR	CONTRIBUTOR and APPROVER
Introduce the business change initiative.	MAJOR	SUPPORTER
Kick-off the design project.	MINOR	SUPPORTER
Train and certify the team.		

SET THE DIRECTION FOR THE BUSINESS PROCESS DESIGN

Establish Business Requirements needed to achieve Business Objectives.	MAJOR	CONTRIBUTOR and APPROVER
Assess Business Policies— current, proposed, and potential areas for change.	MAJOR	CONTRIBUTOR and APPROVER
Develop a Statement of Direction on External and Internal Influences.	MAJOR	CONTRIBUTOR and APPROVER
Establish Design Principles.	MINOR	CONTRIBUTOR
Review direction setting with the team.	MINOR	SUPPORTER

UNDERSTAND YOUR AS-IS BUSINESS PROCESSES

Document the current business processes.		
Validate the processes.		

DESIGN THE TO-BE BUSINESS PROCESSES

Outline the high-level processes of the To-Be design.		
Organized the project into chunks of work and launch work packages.		
Design the business processes.	MINOR	CONTRIBUTOR and SUPPORTER
Develop End-to-End process flows to simulate the key business scenarios.		
Insure integrity of the design through integration.		
Develop first cut of where technology enablers can best support the business processes.		

GAIN APPROVAL FOR THE PROPOSED BUSINESS PROCESSES

Prepare for the approval performance.		
Deliver the performance.	MAJOR	APPROVER
Rework the design if necessary.		

EDUCATE YOUR ORGANIZATION

Review the business drivers.		
Hold the education performances.		

Summary of the Executive's Role

It's easy to surmise that you will be in high demand at the beginning since your job is to ensure that the project is well defined, staffed, and launched. Your role in direction setting is crucial to the team starting out with the right expectations and vision. Having contributed significantly to the launch, however, you can confidently stay out of the way and let the team get on with their work. You can choose to play an important role and contribute to aspects of the process design that impact your particular area of responsibility. Most executives, however, choose not to play a major role during design. Instead, they wait until the team is ready to present their first approval performance before getting into the details of the proposed process design.

The rest of this chapter describes in more detail the involvement and role of all executives, whether or not the executive is a member of the Steering Committee. The expanded role of the Executive Sponsor is also shown.

The Executive Role in the Get-Organized-and-Launch Phase

You can see from Table 7.1 that the Program Manager and Executive Sponsor need to invest a good deal of time upfront to ensure that the program is properly defined and launched. The other executives in the organization have key roles to play, but their time commitment is not as intense. An executive's contribution to defining the Business Objectives, Program Objectives, and Program Scope are critical to gaining alignment and launching the entire program in the right direction. Executive time will be needed to participate in facilitated sessions to develop these three key documents.

The other key to success is staffing the Business Process Design Project with the right people. Executives need to understand the level of involvement required for their staff and then commit their resources to fully participate in the activities of the

Table 7.1 The Executive Role in the Get-Organized-and-Launch Phase

Major Activities	Executive Roles and Responsibilities		
	Program Manager	Executive Sponsor	Executive
Clearly Define the Program			
• Business Objectives • Program Objectives • Program Scope	FACILITATOR Works with Executive Sponsor to develop Objectives and Scope. Facilitates sessions with other executives to reach consensus.	MAJOR CONTRIBUTOR and APPROVER Formulates Objectives and Scope. Positions programs with other executives to gain support and approval to proceed.	MAJOR CONTRIBUTOR and APPROVER Participates in facilitated sessions to develop Objectives and Scope. Approve the Scope definition, with full understanding of its impact on executive's areas of responsibility.
• Program Organization	ADMINISTRATOR Ensures all required program positions are staffed.	APPROVER Ensures appropriate executives are committed to actively participating on Steering Committee. Approves program staff appointments.	
• Program Charter	MAJOR CONTRIBUTOR Develops Program Charter in accordance with the direction from Objectives, Scope, and Organization.	APPROVER Approves Program Charter.	APPROVER Approves Program Charter.

Table 7.1   The Executive Role in the Get-Organized-and-Launch Phase *(continued)*

Clearly Define the Business Process Design Project

• Project Objectives • Project Scope	MAJOR CONTRIBUTOR Works with Executive Sponsor to develop Objectives and Scope.	MAJOR CONTRIBUTOR and APPROVER Formulates Objectives and Scope. Positions design project with other executives to gain support and approval to proceed.	MINOR CONTRIBUTOR Contributes ideas for the Objectives and Scope.
• Project Charter	MAJOR CONTRIBUTOR Develops Project Charter in accordance with the direction from Objectives, Scope, and Organization	APPROVER Approves Project Charter.	APPROVER Approves Project Charter.

Select the Business Process Design Team

	ADMINISTRATOR Works with Executive Sponsor to ensure all required positions are staffed.	MAJOR CONTRIBUTOR and APPROVER Commits members of own staff to the project. Ensures other executives are committing appropriate/qualified staff to project. Approves all project staffing appointments to ensure that a strong design team is in place	MAJOR CONTRIBUTOR Commits members of own staff to the project.

Table 7.1 The Executive Role in the Get-Organized-and-Launch Phase *(continued)*

Introduce the Business Change Initiative to the Organization

MAJOR CONTRIBUTOR Develops agenda and chairs the meeting. Presents mostly administrative subjects.	MAJOR CONTRIBUTOR Presents the key messages including Objectives, Scope, and Organization.	MINOR CONTRIBUTOR Presents an executive message about the importance of the change initiative.

Kick-Off the Business Process Design Project

MAJOR CONTRIBUTOR Develops agenda and chairs the meeting. Presents many of the topics, including Objective, Scope, Organization, and project administrative subjects.	MINOR CONTRIBUTOR Presents an executive introductory message including a review of Program Objectives and Scope.	SUPPORTER Optionally attends part of the kick-off.

Train and Certify the Team

ADMINISTRATOR Ensures all required team members are trained and certified.		
Program Manager	**Executive Sponsor**	**Executive**

design project. Here's a simple rule in assigning people to a process design project: *The people you can least afford to give up are the ones that you need to assign to the project.* It's a simple rule, but if it's not followed, the rest of the organization will know it right away. You really need to assign your best resources to a process design project whose goal is to build a new process and systems foundation for your organization's future.

The Executive Role in the Set-the-Direction Phase

Your role as an executive is to be a major contributor to the development of the direction-setting documents. Table 7.2 outlines where your involvement is vital to setting the tone and direction for the change initiative. As both a major contributor and approver of the business requirements and policies, your involvement in facilitated sessions to develop these key drivers is critical. Because these will continue to develop and change as the project progresses, you should expect to participate throughout the project, not just at the beginning to develop the initial cut at requirements and policies.

The Statement of Direction on External and Internal Influences also requires your participation. The direction set by this document will either shorten the time that the team may have to spend trying to sort out a myriad of options, or it will launch them into research and analysis of the various ways to structure processes and enabling systems. Because this document is so influential, it's important that you contribute your thinking to its development.

Diagram 7.1 shows the development of the different documentation required for the program and the Business Process Design Project. It's important to see the difference between the direction-setting documents that are needed early on to guide and launch the program and its first project, and the documentation that the team will develop and deliver later as part of their design work.

Table 7.2   The Executive Role in the Set-the-Direction-Phase

Major Activities	Executive Roles and Responsibilities		
	Program Manager	Executive Sponsor	Executive
Develop Direction-Setting Documents			
• Business Requirements • Program Policies • Statement of Direction on External and Internal Influences	ADMINISTRATOR Ensures all direction-setting documents are developed and distributed.	MAJOR CONTRIBUTOR and APPROVER Participates in facilitated sessions to develop the direction-setting documents. Approves all direction-setting documents. Continues to participate, when required, throughout the project to develop and approve new policies and business requirements.	MAJOR CONTRIBUTOR and APPROVER Participates in facilitated sessions to develop the direction-setting documents. Approves all direction-setting documents. Continues to participate, when required, throughout the project to develop and approve new policies and business requirements.

Table 7.2   The Executive Role in the Set-the-Direction-Phase *(continued)*

Develop Design Principles

FACILITATOR	MAJOR CONTRIBUTOR and APPROVER	MINOR CONTRIBUTOR
Works with Executive Sponsor and design team to develop principles that will guide the team's design work.	Participates in facilitated sessions to develop the design principles. Approves the design principles.	Contributes ideas on the principles. Provides feedback on the ideas of others.

Review Direction Setting with the Team

MAJOR CONTRIBUTOR	MINOR CONTRIBUTOR	SUPPORTER
Develops agenda and chairs the meeting. Presents most of the material to the team. Facilitates discussion with the team.	Participates in question-and-answer session on the direction-setting documents.	Optionally attends part of the direction-setting meeting.

Diagram 7.1   Relationship of the Direction-setting Documents to the Resulting Project Documentation

The Program Manager and Executive develop these high-level documents to provide the entire organization with a better understanding of what the program and the first project are all about.

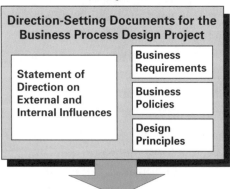

The Program Manager and Executive develop these documents to provide the design team with a better understanding of what the Business Process Design Project is all about and to provide a direction to their work.

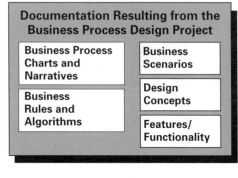

The design team develops these documents as a result of all their work during the Business Process Design Project.

The Executive Role During the Design of the To-Be Business Processes

Some executives can really get into the details of a business process. If you have this ability, then you can make a difference to the design in its early stages. Arrange with the Process Team Leaders to give you enough notice for design review sessions where you can participate and contribute ideas to the design. Your input can usually provide clarity to the team on issues and alternatives that they are considering. By participating here, you can see if the direction given to the team is being followed as you had envisioned. Insight into the process details will also give you a better feeling for new or modified policies. If you can participate at this level of detail, then you can impact the design as it develops.

If you feel that you do not have the talent or time to participate in the early stages of the design, there is still something that you can do to contribute. Just dropping in during a design session can give the team a boost. Executives do not realize that simply coming into a session for 10 minutes and lending their encouragement can go a long way towards showing support for the team. If you're not comfortable participating, just drop into a design session as an observer. It may sound too simple, but try it and discover firsthand the effect your visit creates.

The Executive Role in Approval of the Proposed Business Process Design

Only with sufficient understanding can you approve the design and proceed to the next phase with confidence. It's important to realize that this is not the only point at which you will be asked to approve the design. The approval that you give at this point will take the design out of the mode of the Business Process Design Project and into the next project of the program. This next project could be the technology selection and acquisition, or, if the technology has already been purchased, it could be the conference room pilot. This pilot will test the ability of the technology enablers to successfully support the process flows. As an executive you will also be involved in an approval point at the end of the pilot. If the program is structured correctly, you will continue to have approval points along the way as the various projects of the program are conducted.

To approve the proposed design, you are expected to actively participate and make decisions during the performances of the business processes. You have the final approval for completing the Business Process Design Project. If during a performance or a design review session you feel that rework is required, then you have the prerogative and obligation to request it. After the rework is done, there more than likely will be a need for further design reviews and performances. Do not let the program move into the next phase until the key stakeholders and the Steering Committee are in agreement with the design. They all need to give their explicit approval before the program proceeds to the next step.

The team expects you to become engaged enough in the design to be able to see where the issues and problems might lie. Do not wait until the program "goes live" to say, "Oh, that's not what I expected to see!" This approval step should allow you to achieve a level of understanding where you can articulate your concerns for the new or modified business process that the team is proposing. The team expects and needs your comments to direct them during any rework. Actively participate during the performance of your business processes. Ask questions and make sure the answers are acceptable. Do not hesitate to ask for rework, no matter how small the issue. Everyone involved in a large design project wants the understanding to be thorough and the design to be robust. You have an important role to play in achieving this goal.

The Team's Role in PeopleFlow

Take a look at what your team will actively be doing and developing during the Business Process Design Project. This chapter outlines the key pieces of documentation that the team will develop and deliver over the course of the project. It's important to treat this documentation as a valuable asset within your organization.

The Team's Activities in a Business Process Design Project

GET ORGANIZED AND LAUNCH

	Process Team Leader's Role	Team Members' Role
Clearly define the program.		
Clearly define the Business Process Design Project.	SUPPORTER	
Select the business process design team.	SUPPORTER	
Introduce the business change initiative.	AUDIENCE	
Kick-off the design project.	PARTICIPANTS	
Train and certify the team.	PARTICIPANTS	

SET THE DIRECTION FOR THE BUSINESS PROCESS DESIGN

	Process Team Leader's Role	Team Members' Role
Establish Business Requirements needed to achieve Business Objectives.	MINOR CONTRIBUTOR	
Assess Business Policies— current, proposed, and potential areas for change.	MINOR CONTRIBUTOR	
Develop a Statement of Direction on External and Internal Influences.	MINOR CONTRIBUTOR	
Establish Design Principles.	MINOR CONTRIBUTOR	
Review direction setting with the team.	PARTICIPANTS	

UNDERSTAND YOUR AS-IS BUSINESS PROCESSES

	Process Team Leader's Role	Team Members' Role
Document the current business processes.	MAJOR CONTRIBUTOR	
Validate the processes.	MAJOR CONTRIBUTOR	

	Process Team Leader's Role	Team Members' Role

DESIGN THE TO-BE BUSINESS PROCESSES

	Process Team Leader's Role	Team Members' Role
Outline the high-level processes of the To-Be design.	MAJOR CONTRIBUTOR	
Organize the project into chunks of work and launch work packages.	MAJOR CONTRIBUTOR	
Design the business processes.	MAJOR CONTRIBUTOR	
Develop End-to-End process flows to simulate the key business scenarios.	MAJOR CONTRIBUTOR	
Insure integrity of the design through integration.	MAJOR CONTRIBUTOR	
Develop first cut of where technology enablers can best support the business processes.	MAJOR CONTRIBUTOR	

GAIN APPROVAL FOR THE PROPOSED BUSINESS PROCESSES

	Process Team Leader's Role	Team Members' Role
Prepare for the approval performance.	MAJOR CONTRIBUTOR	
Deliver the performance.	MAJOR CONTRIBUTOR	
Rework the design if necessary.	MAJOR CONTRIBUTOR	

EDUCATE YOUR ORGANIZATION

	Process Team Leader's Role	Team Members' Role
Review the business drivers.	MAJOR CONTRIBUTOR	
Hold the education performances.	MAJOR CONTRIBUTOR	

Summary of the Team's Role

From the above table, you can easily see that the team conducts the design work after the executive sets the direction for the project. The team carries out all the tasks for the As-Is and To-Be design work. A key part of their work is to develop the documentation of the business processes that will continue to be used long after the finish of this project. The team is responsible for preparing and performing the approval performances for the executive. Rework is common, as are subsequent approval performances. The team also needs to be involved in educating the rest of the organization after the Business Process Design Project is finished.

Documentation Developed by the Team

Documentation is an asset. Add up all the time that people in your organization will be spending on the Business Process Design Project and convert it to dollars. Now add to that sum the fees for any outside resources that will be used on the project. It's easy to conclude that the resulting design is a valuable asset to your organization. Capturing and protecting that asset should be a priority. The deliverables of your Business Process Design Project should be treated as a valuable asset. What makes up these assets? Below is a list of the types of documentation that your design team will generate during the project:

- Business Process Charts and Narrative
  - Level-0 Chart (The Context Chart)
  - Level-1 Chart (The Wiring Diagram)
  - Level-2 Charts (The Centre-of-the-Universe Charts)
  - Level-3 Charts (The business processes depicted in a "swim lane" style.)
  - Level-4 Charts (The Level-3 charts expanded to include more details.)
  - End-to-End Charts

- Business Rules, Decision Tables, and Algorithms

- Design Concept Diagrams and Narratives

- Business Scenarios

- Timelines

- Assumptions

- Features and Functionality

This chapter describes an overview of the key business process charts that your design team will deliver. To read further about these charts and to see examples of them, look at Appendix D on page 181. Also in Appendix D are further descriptions and examples of the other types of documentation, listed above, that are required to fully describe business processes. The PeopleFlow practitioner's guide will take your team through the details of creating, developing, and producing this documentation.

Charts Provide the Visual Logic of the Design

Business processes are best documented by representing them visually in charts and diagrams. The logic and flow of the process are the key to its understanding. Charts provide the most cost-effective method of depicting business processes. Software drawing packages allow a business analyst to create charts that communicate the message of what the business process does and how it is accomplished. Charts are not the only method for describing business processes, but they provide the foundation for documenting business processes in a PeopleFlow-driven project. PeopleFlow uses various levels of charts. These levels are used to "peel the onion"—the layers of detail and types of information implicit in the business process. As you look at a set of well-designed charts, you will be easily guided deeper into the structure of the process design.

Business processes are basically a number of activities that are linked together by flows of information, products, equipment, and money. Information flows are common links that one business activity generates and sends on to another activity to be further processed. Physical movements include products that are manufactured, stored, picked, packed, and then shipped from the warehouse to a customer. Money is transferred between businesses to pay for the flow of products and services. The flow of these four elements is represented by lines on the process charts. Every line needs to be labelled with what it represents. Too often lines are not labelled on charts and their significance is left up to you to imagine.

Charts should guide your eye through the flow and allow you to grasp what activities are happening, who is conducting them, and what links them together to form a business process. Other important factors depicted on charts are decisions and escalations that send process flows off in multiple directions, and triggers that initiate activities throughout the process.

The activities of a business process can be classified as manual or technology enabled. A business process can be accomplished by manual labour alone, automation alone, or a mix of the two. The process chart needs to depict the roles of people and technologies conducting manual and automated activities.

Narratives

Narratives will help you during a walk-through of the charts. Although charts should be self-explanatory, an accompanying narrative is a useful aid as you walk through the charts. The process of writing narratives helps the team solidify their understanding of the design. A brief narrative for each chart makes it easier for a wider audience to understand the processes.

High-Level Process Design Charts

High-level charts are used to provide context to the Business Process Design Project and to guide the integration of the design work as it tackles all the various business processes making up the scope of the project. These charts provide an overall perspective of the program and the relevant business processes. The high-level charts include Levels 0, 1, 2, and End-to-End charts.

The Level-0 chart is referred to as the Context Chart.

The objective of the Context Chart is to show a simple yet concise process view of the organization. Executives can use this high-level chart to explain the context of a particular change initiative to anyone inside or outside their organization. It shows the processes included in the scope of the Business Process Design Project and their relationship to the rest of the processes in an organization.

The Context Chart should be developed as the organization's ongoing guide to depict each change initiative as it is formulated. You do not need to develop a new format for the Context Chart every time you start a new Business Process Design Project. Your organization should have a Context Chart format that can be used to launch all your new projects. It should act as your blueprint to the future of process development and technology deployment. In order to play this role, the Context Chart needs to be developed with the participation of all members of the executive. It needs to be a fair representation of all parts of your organization. The Context Chart should be simple and comprehensive. An executive should be able to explain it to customers, suppliers, or employees. Ownership of the Context Chart is at the executive level.

The Level-1 Chart is called the Wiring Diagram.

This is a high-level chart used by the Integration Team, and all process design teams, to ensure that the work stays integrated as the design develops and changes. Without this diagram to guide the integration effort, it is difficult to visualize the integration issues of the processes. Things can easily fall between the cracks without this integration aid.

The Level-2 Charts are called Centre-of-the-Universe Charts.

These charts focus on each major process and help to define the various design teams' area of responsibility. Each design team puts their major process at the centre of their universe and depicts the other major processes as planets revolving around their sun.

End-to-End Charts link individual processes together to achieve an integrated business process.

Executives favour these charts because it gives them an overall view of their major processes. Their main use is to guide the design teams as they develop the details of their processes. Each of these charts shows the complete flow of a significant business process. For example, the Customer Order Fulfillment process is an integrated business process composed of a number of individual processes that must work together to accomplish the goal of fulfilling the customer's order. Some of these individual processes include Capture Customer Order, Edit Customer Order, Allocate and Release Customer Order, Pick/Pack/Ship, Delivery, and Invoice Customer. These individual processes, and the major activities to accomplish them, all link together in a chain to form the End-to-End process.

Detailed-Level Process Design Charts

Detailed-level charts are used to capture the intricacies of the process design. These charts include Levels 3 and 4.

The Level-3 Charts give an overview of a business process flow.

The intent of Level-3 is to show the summary steps that compose a single business process. The objective is to give a complete overview of the business process.

The Level-4 Charts depict the detailed tasks of a business process.

These are the most detailed charts that the team will develop. At this level of detail, the process activity boxes depict individual tasks, and the technology enabler boxes show specific system components, where possible. This level of detail can be used later for training in the implementation phase of the program. The Level-4 Charts are also used to guide the work during the implementation of the technology in a step called the Conference Room Pilot.

Appendices

APPENDIX A LEARNING MORE ABOUT PEOPLEFLOW

If you are interested in finding out more about PeopleFlow, this appendix gives you more information about contacting Pragmatica and the services that it can provide to help you start to use PeopleFlow in your organization.

APPENDIX B GLOSSARY OF TERMS

There are some terms that are casually used in business process design that are not always clearly defined or understood. This Glossary clarifies key terms.

APPENDIX C QUICK REFERENCE GUIDE TO PEOPLEFLOW

This can be a useful guide as you read about the steps of a Business Process Design Project that is driven by PeopleFlow.

APPENDIX D EXAMPLES OF PEOPLEFLOW DOCUMENTATION

PeopleFlow provides a framework for documenting business processes. This appendix gives you examples of the types of documentation that are produced during a Business Process Design Project. Examples of the documentation discussed in Part II are provided here. The types of documentation and the various levels of process charts are illustrated with supply chain examples. The diagrams in Appendix D can be downloaded from the Wiley website for this book, www.wiley.ca/go/processvisualization.

Appendix A
Learning More About PeopleFlow

Pragmatica licenses the PeopleFlow toolkit to organizations that want to learn quickly and effectively how to apply the concepts of Process Visualization to their major business change initiatives. Before you consider making this commitment, you will want to know more about how it can help your organization get started now on your first project. You also want others in your organization to understand and accept the need to move towards becoming a Process Culture. It is often difficult to accomplish this yourself, so how can you best start the ball rolling? Pragmatica has developed the **PeopleFlow Introductory Workshop** to help you understand more about how PeopleFlow can best be introduced into your organization. We will conduct a two-day assignment with your organization. This will include one-on-one sessions, workshop sessions, and an executive presentation. Over the two days, you will become more familiar with Process Visualization and PeopleFlow. Your people will be involved in a few short sessions over the two days so as not to take up too much of their time. You will know at the end of the two days where PeopleFlow can most effectively be used in your organization right now. The PeopleFlow Introductory Workshop has a few simple steps:

- Review of the technology implementation projects currently underway and planned

- Individual discussions with executives about past and current implementation projects

- Presentation of PeopleFlow to your executive and appropriate staff, with time for discussion and answers to their questions

- Presentation of findings and the recommended approach of where to introduce PeopleFlow into your organization

For further information on setting up a workshop, contact Pragmatica at:

Telephone: 416-523-3220
Fax: 416-691-9811
E-mail: pragmatica@sympatico.ca

What Is Included in a PeopleFlow Licence?

The PeopleFlow licence is a non-exclusive licence for organizations to use for their internal projects. As part of the PeopleFlow toolkit, you will receive:

- Hardcopy and softcopy of the practitioner's guide entitled *PeopleFlow: a Handbook for Crafting Business Processes*. The softcopy is provided so that you can make further copies for your organization's internal use only.

- Softcopy of the *PeopleFlow Business Process Tools and Templates*, a collection of software tools, chart standards, and templates to give your team a quick start to documenting their processes.

- Consulting resources to conduct your initial *PeopleFlow Certification Program*. This program provides training and certification for a process design team. Through certification, team members can be confident that they are prepared to participate in a Business Process Design Project. Pragmatica prepares your process design team for their initial PeopleFlow-driven project.

- Consulting resources to guide your organization as it organizes and launches its first Business Process Design Project.

Assisting You Further with Your First Business Process Design Project

You have followed all the steps to prepare your design team for their first Business Process Design Project. The team is trained and certified, and ready to start. But you may want further support to ensure that the first project is a success. Pragmatica can assist you with consulting services aimed at supporting your design teams and engaging your executive group in their initial Business Process Design Project. Our services include:

- Facilitating executive sessions to define Objectives, Requirements, Policies, and Scope.

- Coaching and facilitating the design teams through the Design Mode and Approval Mode of their first project.

- Coaching the Integration Team to ensure that the business process design remains integrated.

- Supplementing your resources with experienced people who participate as team members and Process Team Leaders on your initial Business Process Design Project.

- Documentation support services that encourage your teams to continue learning how to apply the documentation and charting techniques to depict your business processes with greater clarity.

A Step in the Right Direction

Our goal is to make your business change initiatives and technology implementation programs a success by starting them off in the right direction. Pragmatica is dedicated to making you successful in the first step of your major change and technology initiatives by using Process Visualization to develop and simulate the design during the Business Process Design Project. Launching the implementation the right way—with a process design that is understood and approved by the stakeholders and executive—is critical to a successful implementation. We distinguish ourselves with PeopleFlow. A profile of our clients demonstrates our experience in major multi-national enterprises. We pride ourselves in our ability as a boutique management consulting firm to bring about change in large organizations. We promote client self-reliance through knowledge transfer over the course of our assignments. We use PeopleFlow to give your organization the confidence to progress further along the path to becoming a Process Culture.

Appendix B
Glossary of Terms

This Glossary groups together related concepts rather than listing them alphabetically. The concepts are also ordered chronologically—in the manner that you might think of them when organizing and launching a business change initiative. This method of organization should clarify the relationships of the concepts.

Business Change Initiative

An organization is said to conduct a *Business Change Initiative* when it undertakes to significantly transform the way it conducts business in its marketplace with customers and suppliers, or when it strives to significantly improve its operational effectiveness through structural and process changes. An initiative of this magnitude needs to be designed, approved, and then implemented. The implementation most often involves technologies and systems that will enable the newly designed business processes. To have a chance of being successful, it is commonly accepted that the people, processes, and technology all need to be aligned to support the change initiative. The driver of a change initiative could be technological advancements and/or pressures, and business events within an organization and its marketplace.

Business Model

The term *Business Model* is an expression commonly used to refer to the concepts and approach that an organization is going to follow to conduct its business in the marketplace. It is the roadmap that an organization will follow to conduct its change initiative.

For example, Dell has been described as perfecting a business model that takes advantage of a low-price commodity environment. Its just-in-time inventory replenishment coupled with a make-to-order (customers order by mail, Internet, or telephone) approach allows Dell to benefit from lower inventory costs and component prices. Its main competitor, Compaq, has announced that it will alter its business model away from simply selling personal computers and will instead move more towards the IBM model of offering companies a combination of products and services tailored to their specific needs.

E-commerce has a number of different business models that allow customers to communicate, exchange information, and place orders over the Internet.

How does a business model differ from a strategy? According to Michael Porter, a recognized authority from the Harvard Business School on strategy, "Competitive strategy is about being different. It means deliberately choosing a different set of activities to deliver a unique mix of value." (See Reference article indicated by [4].) A business model is unique only if you are the first organization to develop and implement it. Most often, it's not unique. A business model can be an approach that is successfully used by others and has been accepted as a best practice in its industry.

Objectives

An *Objective* specifies the goals or targets that are to be achieved in order for the business change initiative to be successful. For this to happen, the business, program, and all its projects must achieve their objectives. Objectives need to be measurable in some manner in order to determine if they have been met.

Business Objectives

The business change initiative is undertaken for specific reasons. These reasons are the *Business Objectives* that will in some way enhance the organization, its relationships, and its performance. The business objectives state the targets that need to be achieved by undertaking the change initiative. Some examples of business objectives are: to increase profits by reducing costs, to increase customer service levels to a specified percentage, and to increase capacity in the supply chain without increasing warehouse space.

Program Objectives

The program is the vehicle that the organization uses to conduct the change initiative. *Program Objectives*, therefore, are to ensure that the organization achieves its business objectives. The program could also have further objectives that reach beyond the business objectives. For instance, it could have the objective of creating the technical foundation upon which to build further change initiatives.

Project Objectives

The program is accomplished by conducting a number of projects. Each project has different characteristics, but each one needs to achieve its objectives in order for the program to succeed. The *Project Objectives* clearly state, in measurable terms, what this project must accomplish before it is completed and deemed successful.

Scope

The *Scope* is a statement that describes the breadth of a program or project. It specifies the particulars of what is specifically in-scope, and therefore will be considered in the work, and what is definitely out-of-scope, and therefore will not be considered. A precise definition of the scope is essential in keeping the work on time and within budget. Without a precise definition, "scope creep" can start to occur.

Program Scope

The *Program Scope* is the scope of the entire program and, therefore, of the business change initiative. It needs to be defined so its breadth is sufficient to meet the program objectives. The statement needs to be precise and should contain what is and what is not included in the program. It can be defined using the following headings:

- business units/divisions
- product groups
- services
- geographic locations
- customer groups
- supplier groups
- business processes
- enabling technologies

Project Scope

The *Project Scope* is the scope of each project in the program. For the Business Process Design Project, the statement must indicate which business processes are fully in the scope of the project and are to be redesigned in the To-Be design activities. Also it must indicate which processes will be monitored and potentially impacted by the program. These impacted processes therefore are not to be redesigned or changed unless it is absolutely necessary to accommodate information flows or process flow requirements of the in-scope processes.

Organization

Organization refers to the groups of people that are set up to manage and conduct the business change initiative. The roles of the people are defined next.

Program Organization

The *Program Organization* refers to the body of people who are responsible for the successful undertaking and completion of the business change initiative. The table below shows the various roles that are typically found in a program organization.

Steering Committee	The group of senior executives who have the overall responsibility for managing the program. They normally carry titles such as VP and Senior VP in the organization.
Executive Sponsor	The senior executive(s) whose area of responsibility in the organization is most heavily involved in the change initiative. He or she is usually the stakeholder impacted most by the program. This executive is required to devote the most time and effort to the program, and is required to understand more of the design and implementation details than the other members of the Steering Committee.
Chairperson	The person responsible for conducting regular meetings of the committee. He or she could also be the Executive Sponsor.
Steering Committee Members	Senior executives who are also directly or indirectly impacted by the program. Executives who are required to support the change initiative.
Working Committee (optional)	For change initiatives that are being conducted within large organizations, it is optional to set up a Working Committee composed of executives at the Director level. This committee takes a hands-on approach to the program and its daily/weekly activities. This group meets on a frequent basis and attempts to resolve issues and concerns before they reach the level of the Steering Committee.

Program Director	The executive charged by the Executive Sponsor to ensure that the program is staying on track and that business issues and roadblocks are being effectively removed.
Working Committee Members	Directors who have immediate-reporting staff members working on the project teams. As individuals, they report to the executives who form the Steering Committee.
Program Manager	The person responsible for the administrative operation and management of the entire program. Responsibilities include managing the program budget, monitoring all the project's timelines, and ensuring proper resources are allocated to each project. This person reports to the Program Director or Executive Sponsor and reports the status of the project to the committees. For large programs, a Program Management Office may be required to support the Program Manager.

Project Organization (for the Business Process Design Project)

The *Project Organization* refers to the group of people who work on each of the projects in a program. The table below shows the various roles that are typically found in a Business Process Design Project. Other projects in the program will have different roles.

Project Manager	The person responsible for the administrative operation and management of a particular project. Responsibilities include managing the project budget, monitoring the project's timeline, and ensuring that proper resources are allocated during the project. This person reports to the Program Manager. This position is required on all projects in the program.
Integration Team Leader	The person responsible for ensuring that the business processes being designed by the individual process teams all remain integrated. This means that the teams are all designing their Level-3 and Level-4 process flows to fit the design of the End-to-End charts. This person also ensures that all teams uniformly define and use information flows between the major processes. This person reports to the Program Director. On smaller design projects, this person could also take on the role of Project Manager.
Process Team Leaders	Each process stream or major business process that is found on the Context Chart needs a team leader to head up the business process design work. This person is responsible for the design content of his or her business process.

Business Process Analysts	Reporting to the Process Team Leader, these team members are from the business side of the organization. They are responsible for the process design and documentation of their major business process.
Information Technology Analysts	Reporting to the Process Team Leader, these team members are from the technology side of the organization. They are responsible for working on the team to contribute to the process design and documentation. They play a key role in ensuring that information flows are consistent within the major process and that the flows connect correctly to the other major processes. These people can also help to determine and recommend the technologies that should be considered to enable their major business process. From a functional perspective these people will also report to a manager in the IT group, but they are responsible to the Process Team Leader for their work on the project.
Subject Matter Experts	These people are from the business side of the organization and are very familiar with the current business processes and the marketplace. They are called upon by the design teams, as required, to help them understand and validate the As-Is business processes, and to act as sounding boards for design ideas that are being considered for the To-Be process design.

Business Requirement

A *Business Requirement* is a statement about a particular aspect of what the organization needs to have in operation to successfully achieve its business objectives. An extensive list of business requirements is needed in order to specify what the executives wish to have and think they need to have in order to accomplish their business objectives. Requirements sometimes refer to a best practice or a technology that needs to be implemented.

Ask yourself this question to help specify your business requirements:

What do we need to do in order to achieve our business objectives?

Business requirements are direction setting because they emphatically state the specifications that the design needs to achieve in order to be judged as successful. They set the bar and express in business terminology what senior executives are looking for. They become the criteria that the design must meet in order to gain approval. These requirements also give the different process teams working on various aspects of the design a consistent set of specifications that assist in achieving an integrated design. The requirement statements can prevent a design team from going off on a tangent.

Some examples of business requirement statements are:

- Customers will be able to continue ordering product from us by Electronic Data Interchange (EDI), telephone, and fax. We need to expand these current modes to include an Internet order entry and inquiry capability. Also, we need a Vendor Managed Inventory (VMI) capability for our largest customers and fastest-moving items.

- E-Commerce transactions will be expanded to include invoicing and Electronic Funds Transfer (EFT). Our industry is quickly moving further into electronic transactions, and we will continue to be viewed as an early adopter.

- Evaluated Receipt Settlement (ERS) is a best practice that will be designed and piloted in one division before migrating it throughout the organization.

Business Policy

A *Business Policy* is a statement that directs the appropriate range of behaviour for an organization to follow when dealing with the activities and actions of internal people, external people, systems, and other organizations that are suppliers and customers. A policy is a summary statement about the course of action that the organization has chosen to follow in a given circumstance. A policy is used to guide decisions and resolve conflicts. It may incorporate a requirement or a list of rules that clearly dictate the intent and resolve of the organization. It can also be softer and indicate a preferred direction that the organization would like to see followed. Sometimes, business policies that are internal to an organization are referred to as Business Rules.

Three examples of Business Policies are:

1. This example of a policy statement includes specific business rules for suppliers of product to follow. All vendors providing the corporation with product for resale are required to send an electronic version of an Advanced Ship Notice (ASN) to the corporation. The ASN must arrive at least one hour prior to the goods arriving at any corporate or third-party facility. The corporation reserves the right to refuse a shipment if the corresponding ASN has not been received.

2. This example shows how a business requirement drives the need for a business policy directed to external organizations.

The business requirement is: All products moving through the Cross Dock Channel will be scanned into the facility and tracked using the industry standard Serialized Shipping Container Code (SSCC) labels. No other method will be used to handle products flowing through this channel.

The business policy required is: Vendors will only be certified to ship their product through the Cross Dock Channel if they have the capability to pick and pack the shipping containers by store, and then, to label them using the industry standard SSCC label.

3. This example of a policy is softer in nature than the others. Some policies need to be left open to interpretation. The business policy is: We will treat our customers in a fair and equitable manner in the event of a product shortage. We will inform customers as soon as possible about a potential shortage situation of product codes marked critical. We will advise on an estimated time to resolve the situation. During a shortage situation, customer orders that have already been received will be rationed so that each customer is able to receive some quantity of product.

Design Principles

A *Design Principle* is a statement about a fundamental approach or foundation that the program will endeavour to use as the basis for the design. Design principles are those high-level statements that the design team will strive to meet. They are ideals, and if they can be achieved or even approached, then the likelihood of achieving an inspired design is increased. Some people call these "motherhood and apple pie" statements and do not want to bother with them. But design principles can be very useful during the project because they can act as a sounding board against which to test a design or design alternatives. Design principles endure throughout the program whereas the business requirements can often be changed and enhanced. The design team and the Steering Committee contribute their ideas and establish the principles that the program and its projects will follow. When the design team or the Steering Committee are faced with making a decision on which alternative way to proceed, having the design principles to test against can be a logical lifesaver.

As the design project progresses, it is often helpful to match up the design to the design principles. This is especially helpful when informing other people in your organization who are not directly involved in the project how the design is unfolding. Some supply chain examples of design principles are:

- Unbundle the business events, and their dependencies and chronologies, wherever possible. This results in greater process flexibility. It also allows the business processes to be implemented using configurable systems.

- Pipeline Optimization will be the key driver in planning decisions. Optimization means minimizing the total cost to move product through the supply chain and get it to the customer.

- Provide Visibility of Information to all participants in the supply chain with the intention of enhancing decision-making and increasing supply chain effectiveness.

- Simplify and Standardize processes and practices wherever possible. Only add complexity to the design when it is the only means to deliver significant benefits to the program.

Appendix C
Quick Reference Guide to PeopleFlow

The Quick Reference Guide on the following page is useful as you read about the steps of a PeopleFlow-driven Business Process Design Project. The Quick Reference Guide can be downloaded from the website for this book, www.wiley.ca/go/processvisualization.

Quick Reference Guide to PeopleFlow

Get Organized and Launch

Executive's responsibilities
- Clearly define the program that drives the business change initiative
- Clearly define the initial Business Process Design Project
- Select the process design team members
- Introduce the change initiative to everyone
- Kick-off the Business Process Design Project

Team's responsibilities
- Attend team training and achieve certification

Understand As-Is Business Processes

Executive's responsibilities
- None

Team's responsibilities
- Document the current As-Is processes in the scope of the project
- Validate the processes with users and managers

Set the direction for the Business Process Design Project

Executive's responsibilities
- Define the Business requirements needed to achieve the Business Objectives
- Define the Business Policies--current, proposed, and potential changes
- Define a Statement of Direction on External and Internal Influences
- Define a set of Design Principles to guide the program
- Review the direction setting with the design team

Team's responsibilities
- Understand the directions set by the executive and the key documents

High-Level Direction-Setting Documents for the Program

Business Objectives

Program Objective Scope

From direction-setting documents to project documentation.

Business Process Design Project Objective Scope

Direction-Setting Documents for the Business Process Design Project

Statement of Direction on External and Internal Influences

Business Requirements

Design Principles

Business Policies

Documentation from the Business Process Design Project

Business Process Charts and Narratives As-Is To-Be

Business Rules and Algorithms

Feature/ Functionality

Design Concepts

Business Scenarios

People*f*low

Design the To-Be Business Processes

Executive's responsibilities
- Contribute ideas to the new process design
- Support the team members as they work through issues
- Remove roadblocks as the design progresses
- Be prepared to modify policies and requirements, if necessary

Team's responsibilities
- Outline the high-level processes of the new
- To-Be design
- Organize the project into chunks of work and launch work packages to control the different parts of the design
- Design the new business processes using PeopleFlow techniques
- Develop the End-to-End process flows and the various levels of detail for the design
- Insure the integrity of the design by applying the integration techniques
- Develop a first cut of where technology enablers can best support the business process design

Gain Approval for the To-Be Process Design

Executive's responsibilities
- Attend all the performances
- Ensure that you clearly understand the new design
- Call for clarification if parts of the design do not make sense
- Call for rework of the design if parts of it are not right in your estimation
- Give your approval so that the design can be taken to the next step, the implementation of the technology

Team's responsibilities
- Prepare scenarios for the approval performances
- Rehearse for the performances
- Give the performances for the executive and stakeholders
- Rework parts of the design if required by the executive

Influences that impact the Business Process Design Project

INITIAL THOUGHTS ABOUT OUR SYSTEM AND TECHNOLOGY DIRECTION
- Current thinking about how to enable the business processes
- Involvement of Legacy systems

OUR DIRECTION-SETTING DOCUMENTS
- Business Objectives
- Program Objectives
- Business Requirements
- Business Policies

INDUSTRY BEST PRACTICES
- Proven Business Processes
- Standard Practices

BUSINESS DEMANDS BY OUR CUSTOMERS AND SUPPLIERS
- Pressures for new business relationships and technologies to make the industry more effective

BUSINESS PROCESS DESIGN PROJECT and TECHNOLOGY IMPLEMENTATION PROJECTS

INDUSTRY STANDARDS IN TECHNOLOGY
- Protocols and Standards

DIRECTIONS OF OUR INDUSTRY AND COMPETITORS
- Emerging directions and relationships in our industry

NEW AND UNPROVEN CONCEPTS; LATEST THINKING IN THE LITERATURE

PACKAGED SOFTWARE
- Integrated ERP Packages
- Best-of-Breed

EMERGING TECHNOLOGIES
- Industry Exchanges
- Internet Technologies
- Wireless Devices

Appendix D
Examples of PeopleFlow Documentation

PeopleFlow has developed a style of documenting Business Process Design Projects that is comprehensive and intuitive to follow. The **PeopleFlow Business Process Tools and Templates**, a collection of diagrams, chart standards, and templates gives your team the formatting standards for all the document types. Listed below is the documentation that is illustrated or discussed in this Appendix:

- Business Process Charts and Narrative
  - Level-0 Chart (The Context Chart)
  - Level-1 Chart (The Wiring Diagram)
  - Level-2 Charts (The Centre-of-the-Universe Charts)
  - Level-3 Charts (The business processes depicted in a "swim lane" style.)
  - Level-4 Charts (The Level-3 charts expanded to include more details.)
  - End-to-End Charts

- Business Rules, Decision Tables, and Algorithms

- Design Concept Diagrams and Narratives

- Business Scenarios

- Timelines

- Assumptions

- Features and Functionality

High-Level Process Design Charts

These are the first charts to be developed, and they form the foundation for developing the detailed-level charts. The high-level charts include Levels 0, 1, 2, and End-to-End charts.

The Level-0 chart is referred to as the Context Chart.

Diagram D.1 on page 195 shows the Context Chart for a major supply chain initiative. A program of this magnitude involves the design of business processes from many parts of the organization. This chart shows that the organization views itself in process "streams," such as Supply Chain Planning. The major processes are shown within each of these streams. The unshaded boxes indicate those major processes that are fully in the scope of the design project, while the shaded boxes indicate those processes that are impacted by the new process design.

There are a number of ways to design a Context Chart. The chart in Diagram D.1 depicts only business processes and is not concerned with enabling technologies. Enabling a program of this magnitude involves using numerous application systems including Enterprise Resource Planning (ERP), Advance Planning Systems (APS), Customer Relationship Management (CRM), and the use of technologies such as the Internet and Electronic Data Interchange (EDI). Diagram D.2 on page 196 shows a Context Chart that also includes the technology enablers for the business processes.

When people become familiar with a Context Chart, they often ask the question; "What else does that process include?" They are eager to see the next level of detail. Diagram D.3 on page 197 answers their questions. It starts with the Level-0 Context Chart format with the Level-1 major process streams, and then adds the next level of detail, the Level-2 process descriptions. This Chart shows the sub-processes within the major processes. Breaking down the processes to this level of detail is usually enough to satisfy people's casual interest.

The Level-1 Chart is called the Wiring Diagram.

Although this is a high-level chart, there's no question that it looks complex and detailed. Diagram D.4 on page 198 depicts the Wiring Diagram for the earlier Context Chart in Diagram D.1. Level 1 is used for the purpose of process integration. Lines are used to link processes together with flows of information, products, equipment, and money. Linking the processes together, even at a summary level, results in a tangle of wires.

This diagram is used by the Integration Team and all process design teams to ensure that the work stays integrated as the design develops and changes.

Be thankful that as an executive you are not going to be asked to explain the Wiring Diagram to anyone! If you have an opportunity to stand in front of an enlarged version of this chart and follow some of its flows, you'll notice how it all starts to make sense.

The Level-2 Charts are called Centre-of-the-Universe Charts.

There is a Level-2 chart for each major process. These charts help to define the various design teams' area of responsibility. A major process is placed at the centre of the chart and the other major processes are placed around it. A project with the magnitude shown by the Context Chart of Diagram D.1 on page 195 could have one Integration Team and five teams responsible for each of the five process streams. Diagram D.5 on page 199 shows a Centre-of-the-Universe Chart for one major process. The next level of detail, the sub-processes, is shown within the major process of the Level-2 chart. The sub-process is the level at which the team members will do the detailed charting and documentation. The information flowing on the lines linking major processes and sub-processes will increase in level of detail from that depicted on the Wiring Diagram. The Level-2 chart is used by each Process Team Leader to ensure that the design work produced by their team stays integrated within the team, and with all the other processes that link into their processes.

End-to-End Charts link individual processes together to achieve an integrated business process.

End-to-End charts help prevent the teams from thinking and designing in a silo. These charts are used to guide the design teams as they develop their detailed process designs. As the name implies, they depict the design of a major business process that achieves a significant business objective. The team uses the charts during the design work to ensure that integrated business processes are achieved. The Process Team Leaders meet and discuss regularly how their detailed designs are progressing in relationship to the End-to-End charts.

When considering the End-to-End processes for a supply chain, you could conceivably argue that there is only one long integrated process that makes up the chain. But it is more common to create End-to-End process definitions that break the chain into logical sequences of processes that achieve a significant business objective. For example, a distributor could define their set of End-to-End processes as follows:

• Customer attraction and retention

• Customer order fulfillment

• Product and Supplier selection and management

• Replenishment of inventory

The End-to-End charts can become quite long. They are very impressive when enlarged and put up on the wall for general viewing. A typical enlarged End-to-End chart for a supply chain process can be 3-feet wide by 15-feet long. It really catches peoples' attention and curiosity, and raises the interest level in the project.

The level of detail used to depict an End-to-End process is the same or higher as on a Level-3 chart. If the chart is drawn in too much detail, the process becomes difficult to follow and unclear. The activity boxes on the chart depict processes that must be further defined by each of the design teams. These boxes are labelled "Process," or by the common name of the process, for example, Receiving Process. It is possible to show technology enablers on this chart, but it's advisable to show the End-to-End process first, without its technology enablers, and then add them in on a copy of the chart.

The End-to-End chart in Diagram D.6 on page 200 shows the Customer Order Management process. Note all the different functional areas depicted by the swim lanes that are needed to successfully complete this integrated process. The solid line near the top and bottom labelled "LOC" is the Line of Contact. The LOC is used to create a swim lane that shows the activities outside of your organization. The "contact" refers to the touch points with customers, vendors, and service providers. These touch points are critical to the design and implementation of an effective business process. How the touch point is enabled will become an important part of the design. As the design develops, these technology enablers can be added to this chart. In Diagram D.6 the three LOCs are used to provide swim lanes for the activities of Customers, the third-party logistics organization providing warehousing and transportation services, and Vendors.

Notice in Diagram D.6 the small flags labelled "Start" and "End." Now follow the activity boxes between these two flags that are joined by the thicker dark grey arrows, ignoring all the other activity boxes. This is the Mainline Path of the process. This is an important concept in PeopleFlow. It is visually strong, so that your eye will go to this flow first. It's analogous to the critical path on a project management chart. Accomplishing the activities on the Mainline Path is most critical to the process being achieved from the Customer's perspective, even though there are other supporting activities that need to happen.

Detailed-Level Process Design Charts

Detailed-level charts are used to capture the intricacies of the process design. These include Level-3 and Level-4 charts.

The Level-3 Charts give an overview of a business process flow.

At Level 3, the charts use the swim lane style to depict the flow of a single business process. The intent of Level 3 is to give a complete overview and show the summary steps that compose a process. The process activity boxes can be made up of specific tasks and sub-processes. Level-3 Charts can optionally show the systems that enable the process. The technology enablers are labelled at a summary description level only. As an executive, you may not want any further detail than that provided by Level 3. If you are interested in more detail about the process, take a further look at Level 4.

An example of a Level-3 Chart is shown in Diagram D.7 on page 202. This chart shows how one of the processes for fulfilling customer orders is achieved through the activities of both your organization and those of a third-party logistics provider (3PL). Note how the two LOCs divide the chart into three major swim lanes. The dashed line labelled "LOA" is the Line of Automation. The lozenge shapes on and below the LOA depict the systems and technologies that enable the process activities. This chart shows the organization's LOA and also the 3PL's LOA. For clarity, it does not include the Customer's LOA, although this could have been depicted also. Notice how the thicker dark gray arrows show the Mainline Path concept as they did on the End-to-End chart. The concept of the Resolution Path is introduced on Diagram D.7. When things go wrong on the Mainline Path, you correct them by following the process activities on the Resolution Path. This path is depicted using the dashed arrows. In many processes, getting the Mainline Path right is fairly straightforward; it is the time and effort spent resolving issues and problems that consume your resources.

The Level-4 Charts depict the detailed tasks of a business process.

At this level of detail the process activity boxes depict individual tasks and the technology enabler boxes show specific system components where possible. Because of their detail, the Level-4 Charts are also used to guide the work during the conference room pilot. During this pilot your teams will be using the actual installed technologies to walk through the process steps and prove that the technology will support the process requirements. You will develop detailed scripts for the pilot based on the Level-4 charts. The time and effort spent in the Business Process Design Project making sure that the Level-4 charts truly depict the To-Be process details will ensure a positive start to your technology implementation.

An example of a Level-4 Chart is shown in Diagram D.8 on page 204. This chart shows the proposed process for fulfilling the request by a consumer for an item that the organization does not stock but still wants to sell to the consumer. Your eye should pick up on the two LOCs that define the three participants, the organization, the consumer, and the vendor. Notice also the two LOAs that show the enabling technologies. The Mainline Path is very prominent on this chart. There is only one Resolution Process shown, although smaller issues could arise when dealing with the consumer.

The process shown in Diagram D.8 indicates the strong impact that the Business Requirements specified by the executive have on the process design. The note at the top of the chart indicates that the first requirement is to have the consumer come to the store to pick up the special order as opposed to sending it out by mail or courier. This requirement is to encourage traffic through the store. The organization wants to provide this special order service only to its established customers. It wants to encourage the consumer to order the item through a store clerk, either in the store or over the phone. The organization does not wish to become a Web site that is a broker for special orders, but rather wants consumers to continue dealing with its people. If either of these two requirements were relaxed, visualize how the changes would affect the process and the look of this chart.

Business Rules, Decision Tables, and Algorithms

Business Rules, Decision Tables, and Algorithms are used to document the more complex parts of process logic. All the intricate logic that is required in a business process cannot be shown on a process chart. Attempts to show complex logic on a chart only result in confusion and loss of clarity. The essence of the process flow can be lost in a myriad of detailed decision diamonds and yes/no arrows.

Complex logic can best be documented using statements about the business rules or decision tables that capture all the various conditions and their resulting actions. Algorithms document mathematical calculations and their accompanying logic. The details of complex logic are, nevertheless, an important part of the design project. Without the logic to drive the process, it would be impossible to build or implement the design. For example, say that you want to implement new pricing logic for your products and customers. You want the new pricing logic to give more flexibility but be simpler than your current logic. There is a pricing process to follow when the pricing logic is being applied to a new or changed customer order that can be effectively shown on a process chart. The actual logic that calculates the price is difficult to convey with a process chart. A different technique is required to clearly document its logic because it involves a host of factors such as multiple discounts, timing of the order, other items on order, and promotional ordering rules.

PeopleFlow has a number of methods to document Business Rules and Algorithms that make it easy to understand the underlying logic. If you are redesigning the logic, you will want to easily compare your current logic to the new logic. The Decision Table, in particular, can be very useful. It lists all the various conditions that can exist and then defines the resulting actions that are allowed. Diagram D.9 on page 206 illustrates a Decision Table with multiple conditions that can occur non-sequentially, and the resulting allowable actions that can be taken by two functional areas of the organization.

Design Concept Diagrams

Design Concept Diagrams show the underpinnings of the design. Design Concept Diagrams are nothing more than schematic drawings that illustrate the designer's view of the underlying concepts that are critical to understanding the design. It is helpful to understand the underpinnings of the design before going further into the processes and logical details. If these diagrams are too cryptic, they will not convey the essence of the concept. PeopleFlow training takes your team through some simple techniques to make business concept charts more meaningful. Team members do not have to be graphic designers to convey the concepts of your design.

Diagram D.10 on page 207 shows a supply chain concept called "multi-leg." Although this concept is easy to understand, it is difficult to enable with existing technologies. It is important to convey the concept to executives before discussing the underlying technology issues. By seeing how customers receive an order that has travelled on a journey of one, two, or three legs, executives can understand the importance of a system that can provide track-and-trace capabilities anywhere in the distribution network. Now, they can understand that most warehouse management systems have strong functionality to manage the Storage Area in a warehouse but lack capabilities to manage the Holding Area. This simple diagram can lead to some interesting design discussions around the multi-leg concept.

Business Scenarios

Business Scenarios document the actual situations that the processes need to handle. It's very important in the Business

Process Design Project to demonstrate that the business processes can handle all the situations that are likely to arise in the real world. Business scenarios document the events and situations that are expected to occur. They are organized to show all the many relevant situations that may arise. Documenting scenarios can also make use of the decision-table format when a number of conditions apply before a scenario is initiated.

Business scenarios can be divided into two categories. The first are the "perfect" scenarios where nothing goes wrong and everything hums along without a hitch. These scenarios form the Mainline Path. The second category contains all the scenarios with "exceptions." These are the scenarios where a problem or issue needs to be resolved in order that a successful conclusion to the process can be reached. The Exception and Resolution Paths handle these scenarios. If you understand the perfect scenarios first, then you can move through all the exceptions and resolutions more quickly.

Diagram D.11 on page 208 illustrates some of the business scenarios that need to be considered in the multi-channel supply chain design. The team has listed all the scenarios that they will need to consider as they work to develop their To-Be designs. In this case, the number of scenarios to be designed multiplies because most scenarios must work in all four of the distribution channels and for all the different classifications of product types. The design may need to be different for each channel and each product type, although many parts of it may be similar.

Diagram D.12 on page 209 depicts various scenarios in the Customer Order Fulfillment process that arise due to customers requesting a certain level of delivery service and the availability of the product to be shipped. Ten different scenarios result, which must be handled by the business process and its enabling systems. Customer Service Reps know that if a customer's request can not be satisfied by one scenario, they should move on to another scenario to satisfy the request. The lower part of this table provides the design team with key process activities, decisions, policies, and information sources. This table of scenarios is developed to guide the design team when they first start to develop their concepts about how many ways there are to satisfy a customer's request. How often have you heard that there are an infinite number of ways of handling a customer's request? After you work through the various situations that can occur, it becomes apparent that only a finite number of scenarios actually exist. With this breakthrough in thinking, and with the ability to visualize all the scenarios on one page, a design team can move forward with their process designs.

Timelines

Timelines provide a key understanding to the process design. Business process charts are drawn with their flows from left to right to convey a sense of time. But sometimes process understanding requires more than just a general sense of time. To fully realize what the design is meant to achieve, you need to see a more precise timing of the key events. Time in a business process can be measured by the day, by the hour, and even by the minute. It can be the most important element in some new designs. In a design where the goal is to significantly reduce lead times, an understanding of how and where this will be accomplished is essential to understanding the design. Timelines can be added to the bottom of a process chart or drawn independently.

Dealing with Assumptions

Assumptions need to be defined, managed, and matured into more definitive statements. An assumption is a statement about a subject, outside the control of the program, that will be accepted as true for the purpose of continuing on with the Business Process Design Project.

Although assumptions are not welcome during a design project, they need to be accommodated and managed. The best way to minimize their impact is to document them and make them visible to everyone. When assumptions are left up to individual teams to resolve on their own, the risk increases that the design will not be consistent or integrated. If one process team is designing under one assumption and another team works away not knowing this assumption or even makes a different assumption, then integration of the design will be difficult. When this happens, rework will be needed to align these different design perspectives into a single integrated design.

Assumptions are documented and managed using an Assumptions Repository. The PeopleFlow practitioner's guide explains the details of documenting and managing assumptions.

Features and Functionality

Features and functionality are the user-friendly aspects of the systems and technology enablers that make it easier for everyone to do a better job. One example of a desired feature might be the ability to see how the price of a product on an order was calculated. When inquiring about a customer's order, you might want to be able to access a product-pricing window that shows how the customer's price was derived, and how all the pricing components and discounts were taken into account.

The emphasis for the process design team needs to remain focused on business processes. However, both the IT and business team members tend to think ahead and question:

- How will the design be enabled?

- How can we make it easier for the people doing the job?

- How can we enable the process so that customers' perception of our organization is enhanced?

- How can we enable this process to add value to the customer?

During the Business Process Design Project, let the process designers generate their ideas on how features and functionality will enhance the process; capture them in a list. The team can capture these initial thoughts using a document called Features and Functionality. With IT representatives working closely with the design team, the initial thinking on enabling business processes starts during the Business Process Design Project. This list of features and functionality is a "parking lot" of ideas that will be taken into the next phase of the program. The PeopleFlow practitioner's guide describes the Features and Functionality Document in more detail.

The diagrams in Appendix D can be downloaded from the Wiley website for this book, www.wiley.ca/go/processvisualization.

Diagram D.1   Level-0 Context Chart for a Business Process Design Project

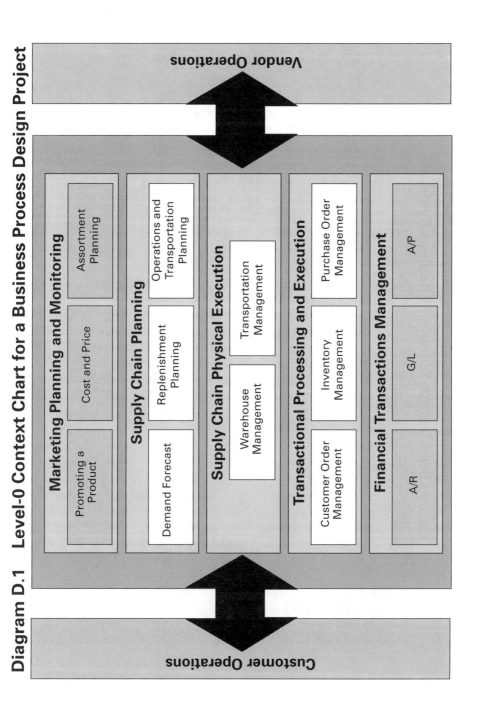

196

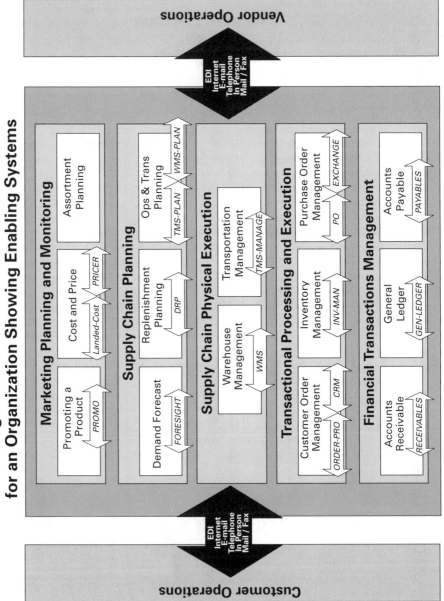

Diagram D.2 Level-0 Context Chart
for an Organization Showing Enabling Systems

Diagram D.3   Context Chart Showing the Next Level of Process Definition Detail for Three Process Streams

Supply Chain Planning

Demand Forecast	Replenishment Planning	Operations and Transportation Planning
(1) New product introduction	(1) Develop import data, run DRP and develop replenishment plan by channel	(1) Warehouse capacity planning
(2) Develop annual marketing forecast	(2) Replenishment exception resolution handling	(2) Transportation capacity planning
(3) Develop promotional forecast	(3) Develop promotional forecast	(3) Direct ship scheduling
(4) Develop and maintain period operational forecast	(4) New product introduction; Changes to source and packaging	(4) Warehouse labour and resources planning
(5) Forecast exception handling	(5) Forecast exception handling	(5) Warehouse and transportation daily scheduling

Supply Chain Physical Execution

Warehouse Management	Transportation Management
(1) Inbound resource execution and management	(1) Inbound/outbound load management
(2) Receiving and putaway	(2) Carrier management
(3) Holding areas management	(3) Carrier operations
(4) Operations support	(4) Fleet management
(5) Outbound resources execution and management	(5) Yard/dock management
(6) Picking locations replenishment	
(7) Picking and shipping	

Transactional Processing and Execution

Customer Order Management	Inventory Management	Purchase Order Management
(1) Order capture	(1) Receipts to inventory	(1) Create P.O. (DRP and manually); Communicate P.O. and P.O. changes
(2) Edit/create/maintain order	(2) Inventory adjustments	(2) P.O. Maintenance and cancel
(3) Executive order handling	(3) Shipments from inventory	(3) Enable inbound process
(4) Customer invoicing	(4) Inter-facility transfers	(4) Enable vendor payment
(5) Customer returns	(5) Inventory valuation	(5) Claims and returns

Diagram D.4   Level-1 Wiring Diagram for the Business Process Design Project

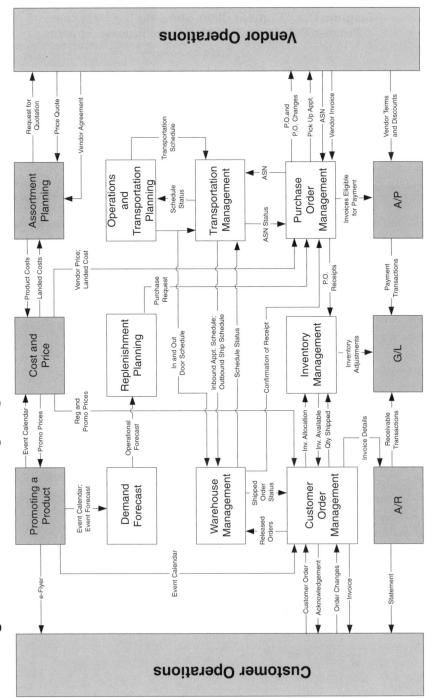

Diagram D.5 Level-2 Chart for Purchase Order Management

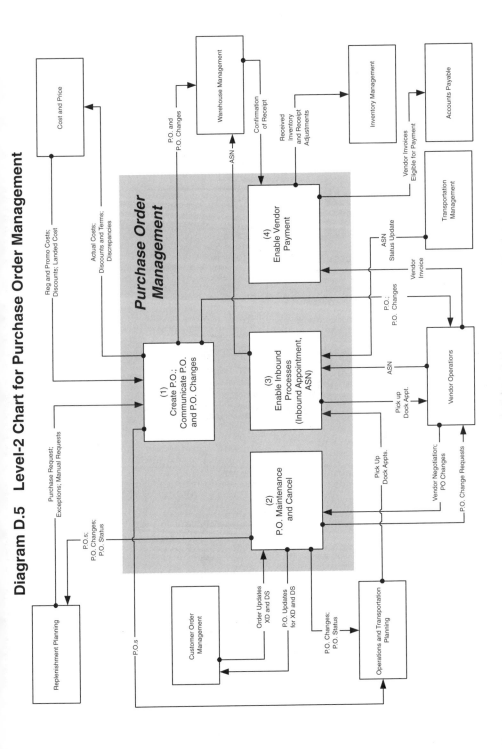

Diagram D.6 End-to-End Chart Showing a Simplified Customer Order Management Cycle

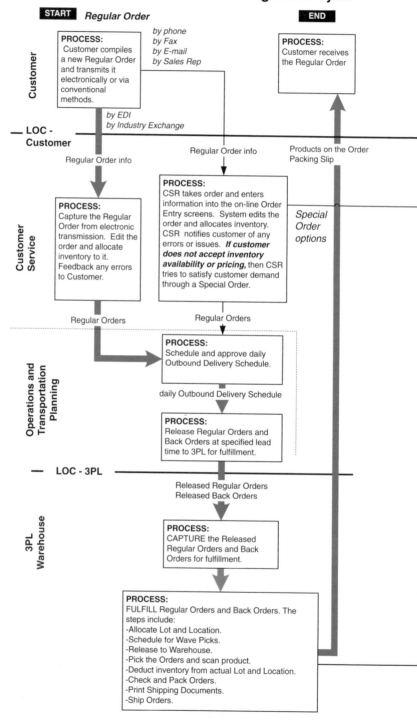

START *Regular Order*   **END**

Customer

PROCESS:
Customer compiles a new Regular Order and transmits it electronically or via conventional methods.

by phone
by Fax
by E-mail
by Sales Rep

PROCESS:
Customer receives the Regular Order

by EDI
by Industry Exchange

___ LOC - Customer

Regular Order info

Regular Order info

Products on the Order Packing Slip

Customer Service

PROCESS:
Capture the Regular Order from electronic transmission. Edit the order and allocate inventory to it. Feedback any errors to Customer.

PROCESS:
CSR takes order and enters information into the on-line Order Entry screens. System edits the order and allocates inventory. CSR notifies customer of any errors or issues. **If customer does not accept inventory availability or pricing,** then CSR tries to satisfy customer demand through a Special Order.

Special Order options

Regular Orders

Regular Orders

Operations and Transportation Planning

PROCESS:
Schedule and approve daily Outbound Delivery Schedule.

daily Outbound Delivery Schedule

PROCESS:
Release Regular Orders and Back Orders at specified lead time to 3PL for fulfillment.

— LOC - 3PL

Released Regular Orders
Released Back Orders

3PL Warehouse

PROCESS:
CAPTURE the Released Regular Orders and Back Orders for fulfillment.

PROCESS:
FULFILL Regular Orders and Back Orders. The steps include:
-Allocate Lot and Location.
-Schedule for Wave Picks.
-Release to Warehouse.
-Pick the Orders and scan product.
-Deduct inventory from actual Lot and Location.
-Check and Pack Orders.
-Print Shipping Documents.
-Ship Orders.

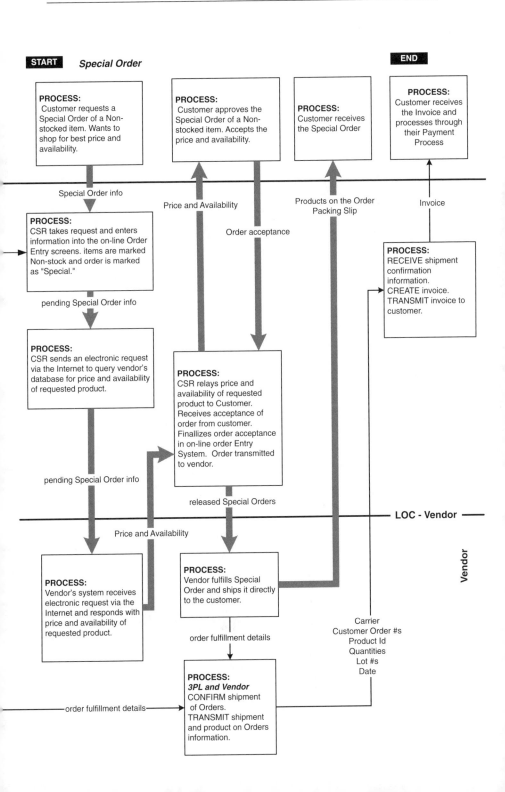

START *Special Order*

PROCESS:
Customer requests a Special Order of a Non-stocked item. Wants to shop for best price and availability.

PROCESS:
Customer approves the Special Order of a Non-stocked item. Accepts the price and availability.

PROCESS:
Customer receives the Special Order

END

PROCESS:
Customer receives the Invoice and processes through their Payment Process

Special Order info

Price and Availability

Products on the Order Packing Slip

Invoice

PROCESS:
CSR takes request and enters information into the on-line Order Entry screens. items are marked Non-stock and order is marked as "Special."

Order acceptance

PROCESS:
RECEIVE shipment confirmation information. CREATE invoice. TRANSMIT invoice to customer.

pending Special Order info

PROCESS:
CSR sends an electronic request via the Internet to query vendor's database for price and availability of requested product.

PROCESS:
CSR relays price and availability of requested product to Customer. Receives acceptance of order from customer. Finallizes order acceptance in on-line order Entry System. Order transmitted to vendor.

pending Special Order info

released Special Orders

LOC - Vendor

Price and Availability

PROCESS:
Vendor's system receives electronic request via the Internet and responds with price and availability of requested product.

PROCESS:
Vendor fulfills Special Order and ships it directly to the customer.

Vendor

Carrier
Customer Order #s
Product Id
Quantities
Lot #s
Date

order fulfillment details

order fulfillment details

PROCESS:
3PL and Vendor
CONFIRM shipment of Orders. TRANSMIT shipment and product on Orders information.

Diagram D.7 Example of a Level-3 Chart Showing Activities and Responsibilities for an Outsourcing Relationship with a Third Party Logistics Provider

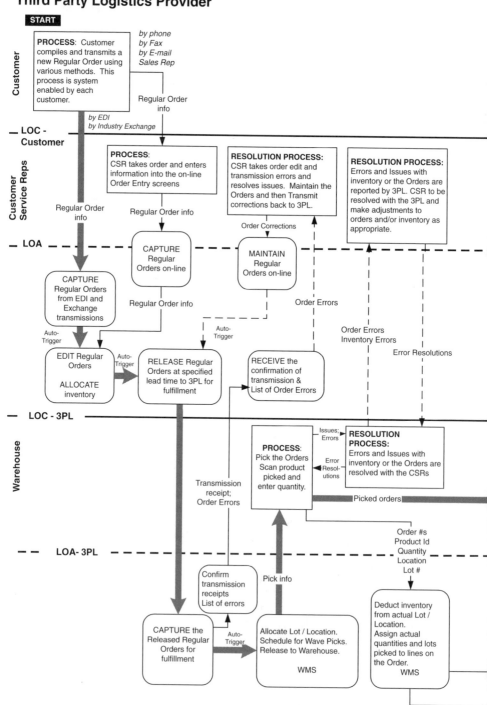

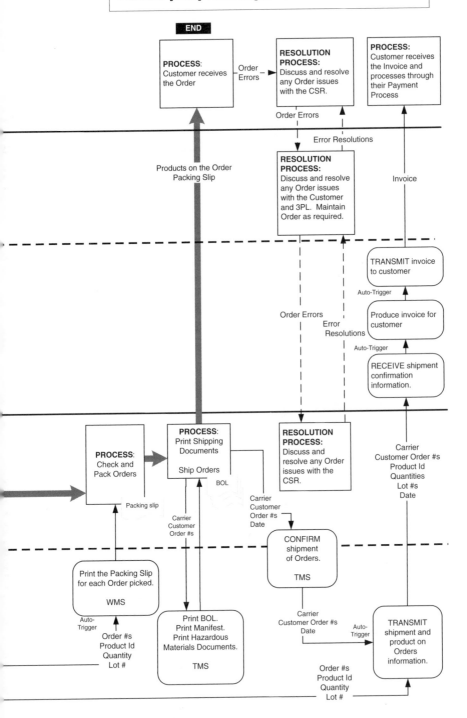

Customer Order Fulfilment To-Be Level-3
Process: [CO.1] Fulfill Regular Orders and Back Orders

Diagram D.8   Level-4 Chart for Customer Order Fulfillment

CO. Customer Order Fulfilment To-Be Level-4
Process: [CO.1.6] E-Fulfill Consumer Special Order

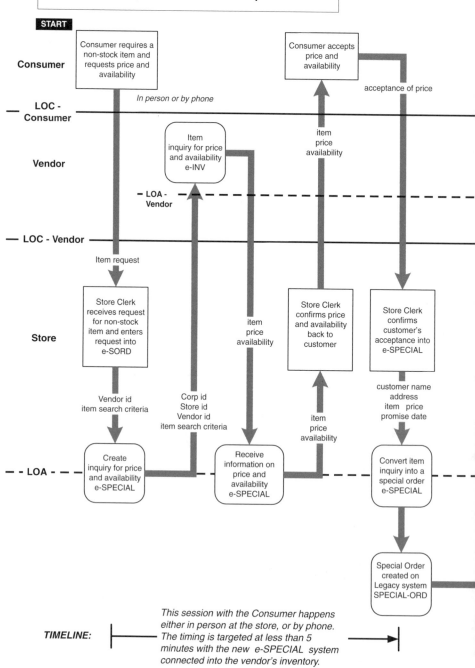

This chart describes one of the proposed methods of fulfilling special orders to consumers through e-fulfilment technology enabled by the Internet. Vendor shipments are direct to store with no HO or warehouse processes involved. The business model still requires that customers pick up the items in person to encourage traffic through the stores. The item can be ordered by the consumer either over the phone or in person, but not over the Internet.
Facilities involved: all stores
SKU's involved: items not stocked at the warehouses.

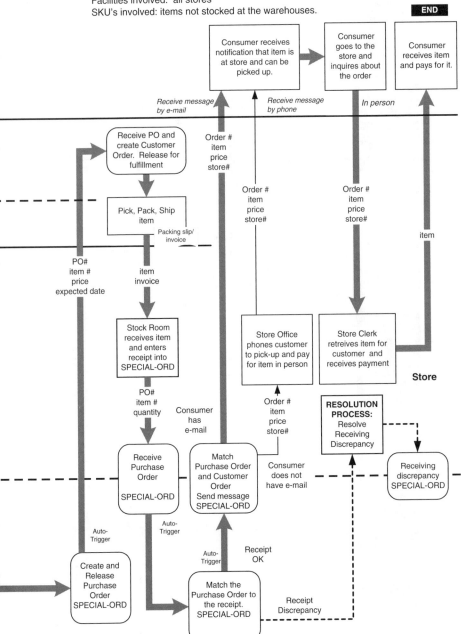

Diagram D.9 Decision Table Showing the Conditions that Trigger Key Supply Chain and Financial Actions for an Inbound Shipment from a Vendor

Non-Sequential Conditions				Supply Chain Actions	Financial Actions
Pick Up Appt. Ok'd	ASN Received	Shipment Arrived	Product Received	Receive into stock / Allocate to orders / Schedule outbound	Payment allowed to vendor
N	N	N	N	No action allowed	No action allowed
Y	N	N	N	No action allowed	No action allowed
Y	Y	N	N	Action allowed if vendor classified "ISO certified"	Action allowed if vendor classified "ISO certified"
Y	Y	Y	N	Action allowed for all vendors	Action allowed for all vendors
Y	Y	Y	Y	Action allowed for all vendors	Action allowed for all vendors
Y	N	Y	N	Action allowed if vendor classified "ISO certified"	Action allowed if vendor classified "ISO certified"
Y	N	Y	Y	Action allowed for all vendors	Action allowed for all vendors

The design team wanted to shrink the lead time for the outbound planning process. They wanted to be able to start allocating stock to customer orders, then schedule the outbound deliveries, even before the product had arrived and was received at the warehouse. This decision table shows when these actions can be taken.

Decision Tables provide the team with a methodical way of ensuring that all the conditions that could possibly happen are accounted for and the appropriate actions specified. When the conditions become numerous, then this format is the most effective to illustrate the logic. These charts are invaluable to the IT team when they have to configure software or design/modify programs. Imagine what a process chart would look like to express all these decision points. It would be too convoluted and would not provide clarity to the logic.

Diagram D.10 Design Concept Diagram Showing Single-Leg and Multi-Leg Movements of Customer Orders

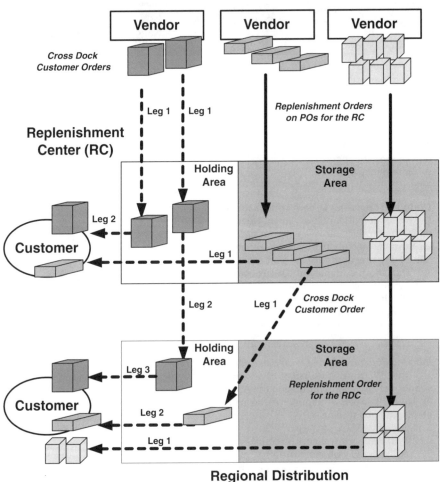

Diagram D.11   Scenarios to be Validated in the Supply Chain Channels

Scenarios	Storage	Flow Through	Cross Dock	Direct Ship
Supply Chain Channels				
The "Perfect" Scenarios with No Exceptions				
1. The "perfect" Regular Customer Order and Purchase Order for product types:				
Regular product	❖	❖	❖	❖
Non-stocked product			❖	❖
Non-listed product			❖	❖
2. The "perfect" Promotion. C.O. and P.O. have no exceptions.	❖	❖	❖	❖
3. Emergency C.O. and P.O.	❖		❖	❖
Outbound Customer Orders with Exceptions				
1. Not enough quantity on-hand. Need to ration the product across customer orders.	❖	❖	❖	❖
2. Stock availability expected later than required to meet promise date on order.	❖	❖	❖	❖
3. Over, short, or damaged (OSD) customer order requires claims process.	❖	❖	❖	❖
4. Substitute product on customer order.	❖		❖	❖
5. Changes and cancellation of customer order lines for regular and promotion items.	❖	❖		
Inbound Purchase Orders with Exceptions				
1. No ASN arrives because of new vendor or vendor not capable of producing the ASN.	❖	❖	❖	❖
2. No ASN arrives on time for Arrivals Process at the gate of a facility.	❖	❖	❖	❖
3. Incorrect ASN	❖	❖	❖	❖
4. Blind Receiving discrepancies:				
>ASN to PO does not match	❖	❖	❖	❖
>Receiving count to ASN does not match	❖	❖	❖	❖
>BOL to ASN does not match	❖	❖	❖	❖
5. Over, Short, Damage (OS), including the wrong product delivered.	❖	❖	❖	❖
6. Non-expected arrival of a shipment for any reason, including from a courier and trailer arriving at wrong facility.	❖	❖	❖	❖

Diagram D.12 Ten Order Fulfillment Scenarios Generated by Differing Ordering Requests (including process activities and policies that apply to each scenario)

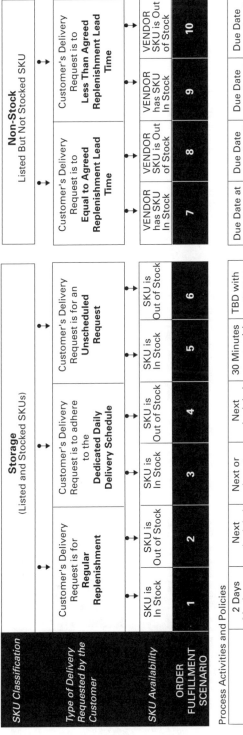

SKU Classification	Storage (Listed and Stocked SKUs)						Non-Stock (Listed But Not Stocked SKU)			
Type of Delivery Requested by the Customer	Customer's Delivery Request is for Regular Replenishment		Customer's Delivery Request is to adhere to the Dedicated Daily Delivery Schedule		Customer's Delivery Request is for an Unscheduled Request		Customer's Delivery Request is to Equal to Agreed Replenishment Lead Time		Customer's Delivery Request is to Less Than Agreed Replenishment Lead Time	
SKU Availability	SKU is In Stock	SKU is Out of Stock	SKU is In Stock	SKU is Out of Stock	SKU is In Stock	SKU is Out of Stock	VENDOR has SKU In Stock	VENDOR SKU is Out of Stock	VENDOR has SKU In Stock	VENDOR SKU is Out of Stock
ORDER FULFILLMENT SCENARIO	1	2	3	4	5	6	7	8	9	10

Process Activities and Policies

Process Activities and Policies	1	2	3	4	5	6	7	8	9	10
Establishing Promise Date and Time:	2 Days Maximum [as per Policy]	Next scheduled run after In Stock	Next or closest scheduled run TODAY	Next scheduled run after In Stock	30 Minutes max to pick and ship as per Policy	TBD with customer	Due Date at warehouse using lead time table	Due Date negotiated with Vendor	Due Date negotiated with Vendor	Due Date negotiated with Vendor
Establishing Price to Consumer:	• Maintained by us. • Available on-line from price database						• Maintained by us. Calculated from vendor cost • Available on-line from price database			
Establishing Cost to Corporation:	• Maintained by us. • Available on-line from cost database						• Maintained by Vendor and transmitted to us • Available on-line from product cost database			
Establishing Availability of SKU	• SKU availability through On-line Inquiry to Corporate Inventory Database						• On-line to Vendor's inventory database • Phone Call inquiry to Vendor			
Establishing Freight Charge:	• Applied using agreed to standards in Customer Contract • Applied to other customers if less than order minimum						• Applied using agreed upon standards in Customer Contract • Applied to other customers if less than order minimum • At customer's expense (only at our expense if due to service failure)			

References

Bauer, Michael J., Charles C. Poirier, Lawrence Lapide, John Bermudez. *E-Business: The Strategic Impact on Supply Chain and Logistics*. Chicago: Council of Logistics Management, 2001.

Champy, James L. "Reengineering or Dead? Don't Believe It: An Interview with James Champy." *Harvard Management Update*, March 1999.

[2]Davenport, Thomas H. *Process Innovation: Reengineering Work through Information Technology*. Boston: Harvard Business School Press, 1993.

Davenport, Thomas H. "Putting the Enterprise into the Enterprise System." *Harvard Business* Review, July/August 1998.

Davenport, Thomas H., and Laurence Prusak. *Working Knowledge: How Organizations Manage What They Know*. Boston: Harvard Business School Press, 1997.

Dixon, Nancy M. *Common Knowledge: How Companies Thrive by Sharing What They Know*. Boston: Harvard Business School Press, 2000.

Eisenhardt, Kathleen M., and Donald M. Sull. "Strategy as Simple Rules." *Harvard Business Review*, January 2001.

[3]Hammer, Michael, and Steven Stanton. "How Process Enterprises Really Work." *Harvard Business Review*, November 1999.

[3]Hammer, Michael. Beyond Reengineering: *How the Process-Centered Organization Is Changing Our Work and Our Lives*. New York: Harper Collins, 1997.

[3]Hartman, Amir, and John Sifonis with John Kador. *Net Ready: Strategies for Success in the E-conomy*. New York: McGraw-Hill, 2000.

[1]Karpinski, Richard. "Don't Get Nike-ed." *Transformation Today, Internet Week Web site (www.internetweek.com)*, March 7, 2001.

[2]Mabert, Vincent A., Ashok Soni, and M. A. Venkataramanan. "Enterprise Resource Planning: Common Myths Versus Evolving Reality." *Business Horizons*, May/June 2001

[2]Nelson, E., and E. Ramstad. "Hershey's Biggest Dud Has Turned Out to Be Its New Technology." *Wall Street Journal*, October 29, 1999, p. A1.

[2]Osterland, Andrew. "Blaming ERP." *CFO*, January 2000.

[3]Ostroff, Frank. *The Horizontal Organization: What the Organization of the Future Looks Like and How It Delivers Value to Customers*. Oxford: Oxford University Press, 1999.

[4]Porter, Michael E. "What Is Strategy?" *Harvard Business Review*, November 1996.

Schrage, Michael. *Serious Play: How the World's Best Companies Simulate to Innovate*. Boston: Harvard Business School Press, 1999.

Schrage, Michael. "Faster Innovation?: Try Rapid Prototyping." *Harvard Management Update*, December 1999.

Sharpiro, Benson P., V. Kasturi Rangan, John J. Sviokla. "Staple Yourself to an Order." *Harvard Business Review*, July 1992.

³Tapscott, Don, David Ticoll, and Alex Lowy. *Digital Capital: Harnessing the Power of Business Webs.* Boston: Harvard Business School Press, 2000.

²Wheatley, Malcolm. "ERP Training Stinks." *CIO Magazine*, June 2000.

Index